What We Believe Together

What We Believe Together

Second Edition

Exploring the "Shared Convictions" of Anabaptist-Related Churches

by Alfred Neufeld

Photography by Merle Good

Introduction by César García

Published in cooperation with Mennonite World Conference

Good Books
New York, New York

Acknowledgments

Bible quotes are taken from the New International Version unless otherwise noted. The author has made slight adaptations to some of the quotations. Scripture taken from the HOLY BIBLE, NEW INTERNATIONAL VERSION. NIV. Copyright © 1973, 1978, 1984 International Bible Society. Used by permission of Zondervan. All rights reserved.

Photo Credits

Front and Back Covers: by Merle Good.
All interior photos by Merle Good.

Good Books books may be purchased in bulk at special discounts for sales promotion, corporate gifts, fund-raising, or educational purposes. Special editions can also be created to specifications. For details, contact the Special Sales Department, Good Books, 307 West 36th Street, 11th Floor, New York, NY 10018 or info@skyhorsepublishing.com.

Good Books is an imprint of Skyhorse Publishing, Inc.®, a Delaware corporation.

Visit our website at www.goodbooks.com.

10 9 8 7 6 5 4 3 2 1

Library of Congress Cataloging-in-Publication Data is available on file.

Cover and interior design by Cliff Snyder

Print ISBN: 978-1-68099-139-0
Ebook ISBN: 978-1-56148-763-9

Printed in the United States of America

What We Believe Together: Exploring the "Shared Convictions" of Anabaptist-Related Churches is published in cooperation with Mennonite World Conference (MWC) and has been selected for its Global Anabaptist-Mennonite Shelf of Literature. MWC urges its member churches to translate and study the book, in an effort to develop a common body of literature.

Mennonite World Conference is a global community of Christian churches who trace their beginning to the sixteenth-century radical reformation in Europe, particularly to the Anabaptist movement. Today, more than 1.7 million baptized believers belong to this faith family. About 66 percent are African, Asian, or Latin American.

MWC represents 101 Mennonite and Brethren in Christ national churches from 57 countries on six continents.

Mennonite World Conference exists to: 1. be a global community faith in the Anabaptist tradition; 2. facilitate community among Anabaptist-related churches worldwide, and; 3. relate to other Christian world communions and organizations.

MWC's General Secretary's office is in Bogotá, Colombia. For more information, visit its website at www.mwc-cmm.org.

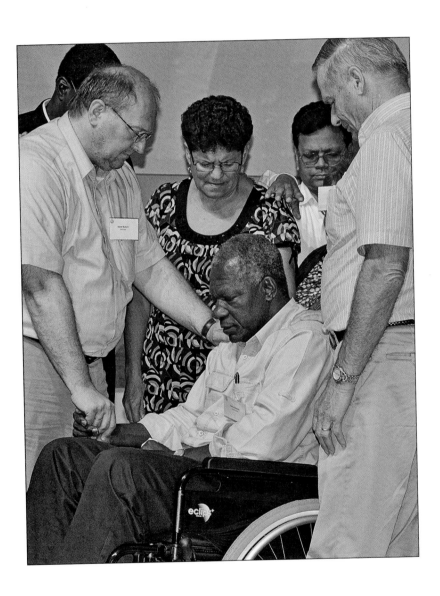

Table of Contents

Introduction

Can we walk together as sisters and brothers? Does Mennonite World Conference (MWC) have a framework that will help us become more interdependent and accountable to each other? These are the kinds of questions that MWC receives from Anabaptist communities who are exploring joining our global family of faith as members.

Mennonite World Conference is a global community of more than 100 national churches who trace their beginnings directly or indirectly to Anabaptism, a movement of reformation in the Christian church of the sixteenth century. Today this movement, with more than 1.7 million baptized members, is present worldwide in more than 80 countries.

Due to the amazing diversity and pluralism that exists in our global body, the questions mentioned above are more than understandable. The "Shared Convictions of Global Anabaptists" is a way of responding to those questions. Larry Miller, former MWC General Secretary, explains how this statement came to be:

> After MWC's Faith and Life Council gathered confessions of faith from member churches, it compared them. Then the Council organized an international body of seven individuals to write a brief, simply stated document of "Shared Convictions."
>
> The statement was digested and discussed by MWC's General Council, made up of representatives from the 97 churches which [at that time] belonged to the MWC community. Over a

three-year period, these delegates, often in consultation with their churches, worked persistently and patiently to reach agreement on a statement that each could heartily claim, and which they could also recommend to their local and national churches.... This statement was received, discussed, and approved by the consensus of the General Council in March, 2006."

MWC's "Shared Convictions" are the result of a process that looked for Anabaptist convictions arising "from below." These "Convictions" are offered both as a *testimony* of our faith walk as a global family, and as a *calling*. They invite conversation with other traditions, and among members of our own. Through them, we hope to explain with humility and clarity our own experience of following Christ.

In this book, Alfred Neufeld, a theologian and professor from Paraguay, offers historical and theological background for these "Convictions," their biblical roots and what it means to practice them today. His rich style and Global-South perspective, along with the study questions prepared by Phyllis Good at the end of each chapter, will help with study, reflection and practice of the "Shared Convictions" in churches around the world.

Can we walk together? Yes—but not because we share a set of theoretical doctrines that we must confess intellectually. Instead, we share convictions that are the fruit of our walk with Christ, as our forebears of the sixteenth century did. You are welcome to join us.

César García,
General Secretary, Mennonite World Conference
Bogotá, Colombia

General Secretary
César García

Statement of "Shared Convictions"

By the grace of God, we seek to live and proclaim the good news of reconciliation in Jesus Christ. As part of the one body of Christ at all times and places, we hold the following to be central to our belief and practice:

1. God is known to us as Father, Son, and Holy Spirit, the Creator who seeks to restore fallen humanity by calling a people to be faithful in fellowship, worship, service and witness.

2. Jesus is the Son of God. Through his life and teachings, his cross and resurrection, he showed us how to be faithful disciples, redeemed the world, and offers eternal life.

3. As a church, we are a community of those whom God's Spirit calls to turn from sin, acknowledge Jesus Christ as Lord, receive baptism upon confession of faith, and follow Christ in life.

4. As a faith community, we accept the Bible as our authority for faith and life, interpreting it together under Holy Spirit guidance, in the light of Jesus Christ to discern God's will for our obedience.

5 The Spirit of Jesus empowers us to trust God in all areas of life so we become peacemakers who renounce violence, love our enemies, seek justice, and share our possessions with those in need.

6 We gather regularly to worship, to celebrate the Lord's Supper, and to hear the Word of God in a spirit of mutual accountability.

7 As a worldwide community of faith and life we transcend boundaries of nationality, race, class, gender and language. We seek to live in the world without conforming to the powers of evil, witnessing to God's grace by serving others, caring for creation, and inviting all people to know Jesus Christ as Savior and Lord.

In these convictions we draw inspiration from Anabaptist forebears of the sixteenth century, who modeled radical discipleship to Jesus Christ. We seek to walk in his name by the power of the Holy Spirit, as we confidently await Christ's return and the final fulfillment of God's kingdom.

Adopted by Mennonite World Conference
General Council
Pasadena, California (USA)
March 15, 2006

Good News

By the grace of God, we seek to live and proclaim the good news of reconciliation in Jesus Christ. As part of the one body of Christ at all times and places, we hold the following to be central to our belief and practice:

Only God's grace enables us

The most amazing miracle, and perhaps the reality most difficult for human beings to understand, is the grace of God. Why should God take interest in arrogant and rebellious human beings?

Why should the good shepherd leave 99 sheep alone and go after the lost one? How is it possible that while on the cross, Jesus reacted with meekness to those who mistreated him?

The apostle John, describing his life with Jesus, said, "We have seen his glory...full of grace and truth. From the fullness of his grace we have all received one blessing after another" (John 1:14-17).

The first person to be enthused about God's grace in the New Testament, together with Zachariah and Elizabeth, was Mary, the mother of Jesus. When she received notice of the role she would play in the history of God's redeeming grace for humanity, she composed a magnificent poem to exalt this grace (Luke 1:30-35).

Grace is the free gift of God's love. It aims at the well-being of humankind, who do not deserve it and are not able to pay for it. The apostle Paul was a violent religious fanatic who persecuted the first Christians. But when he met Jesus Christ, he experienced a radical change. He realized that God's purpose is "to show in the coming ages the incomparable riches of his grace." He discovered that salvation, as well as any good works one does, are results of the intervening grace of God (Ephesians 2:7-10).

St. Augustine from Hippo was a young, brilliant North African of the fourth century. After a disorderly life and a passion for philosophy, he experienced the redeeming work of Christ, thanks to the constant prayers of his mother, Monica. As a prominent teacher of the church he is remembered as the "Doctor of Grace."

Martin Luther was a German monk burdened with feelings of guilt. While studying the theology of Paul, he discovered that what we might be able to achieve does not count in the eyes of God. Even more so, God's grace is enough, because "the power of God is made perfect in weakness" (2 Corinthians 12:9). His large reformation work within the church, which he did together with his wife Katharina, fit within his understanding of *"sola gratia"* or "grace alone."

Menno Simons was a Dutch Catholic priest in the sixteenth century. He performed his priestly duties very superficially, being more attracted to money and card-playing. But when he experienced the transforming grace of God, he, together with his wife Gertrude, became faithful and long-suffering pastors and teachers of the dispersed Anabaptist believers.

Arnold Snyder was the son of Mennonite missionaries to Argentina. Nevertheless, the student revolts of 1968 drew him into rock music and drugs. He experienced change and once told me, "I know what it means to experience God's grace." He became a teacher and researcher of Anabaptist theology. In his book, *From Anabaptist Seed,* written for the Mennonite world family, he summarizes the Anabaptist understanding of grace:

God's grace regenerates former sinners and makes them into new creatures. Believers who have been born again and regenerated by the Holy Spirit have been fitted to interpret and understand God's will in Scripture and to live new lives (page 17).

We seek to live and proclaim good news

If we are true Christians, our lives and our words are inseparable. In fact, our faith and lives will agree to a maximum, so that our communication and our witness have credibility.

The saving grace of Jesus Christ provides salvation and good works, and both are necessary for the proclamation of the Gospel. When God communicated with humankind, it was through deeds and through words. God saved Israel from slavery in Egypt, and gave them a good law of instructions for a new life in the Promised Land. The prophets of God also communicated the message through deeds and through words. Jesus himself gave his disciples "the great commandment" and the "great commission."

Jesus taught that loving God and loving one's neighbor make up the greatest commandment (Matthew 22:37-40). The good news is that God has poured out love into our hearts (Romans 5:5). And the Bible is clear, claiming that love has to do with deeds and not with words (1 John 3:18). Jesus promoted holistic mission and told his disciples, "As the Father has sent me, I am sending you" (John 20:21).

In his great farewell commission (Matthew 28:18-20), Christ sent his disciples to all nations, so that they would make disciples. The commission includes the mandate to baptize, to teach, and to keep the commandments of Jesus. That is why the Christian vocation is both to be and to make disciples.

Reconciliation comes through Jesus Christ

Violence, conflicts, abuses, wars, confrontations, injustice, mutual humiliations—this is the news that invades us daily. Humanity throughout history has had so many bad experiences when trying to solve differences by enmity and vengeance. Yet we seem unable to be cured from this evil.

The Bible tells us, and our experience confirms it, that Jesus Christ makes it possible to overcome hostility and violence. This is the center of the Gospel and of our mission. After the formation of the people of God in the desert, Moses established a great day of reconciliation once a year (Leviticus 23:27). Together with the Jubilee (Leviticus 25:9-10), these celebrations served to establish reconciliation with God and within the community.

With the coming of Christ, the hope of a lasting reconciliation was fulfilled. Jubilee, and the overcoming of hostility, became permanent practices for the community of believers (Luke 4:17-21). The faith community not only aims at being a community reconciled with God and with each other, but it also has received the mission to reconcile. Even more so, God calls the faith community to become an *ambassador* of reconciliation (2 Corinthians 5:14-21).

How is such a high mission actually going to happen? First, the love of Christ is the driving force (verse 14). And the death of Christ frees us to live a life of service (verse 15). Christ also delivers us from prejudice which produces hostility (verse 16). And then, our experience of encountering Christ becomes a creative and transforming force: "So if anyone is in Christ, there is a new creation: everything old has passed away; see, everything has become new!" (verse 17).

Reconciliation grows out of God's mind. When God sent Christ, that initiated the historic process of reconciliation. God took the initiative, so that the world might be reconciled with its Creator. And God gave us the mandate to be a voice of Christ and ambassadors of reconciliation (verses 18-21).

We are part of the one body of Christ

The church of Christ is about to celebrate 2,000 years. On the day of Pentecost, the disciples received power from above, proclaimed the mighty deeds of God in Christ, and baptized a multitude of 3,000. Today, the community of followers of Christ has many faces, different traditions, diverse structures, and multiple ways of articulating and living its faith. Sadly enough, there have also been splits, confrontations, and humiliations among the followers of Christ. So the questions arise: Is it possible to talk of a universal church? Is it possible to talk of just one body of

Christ? And the Anabaptist Mennonite church—is it part of this universal church? If so, what place does it occupy in this one body of Christ? To resolve these questions, we need to remember four truths:

- Since Christ ascended to heaven, God chose the church to make Christ visible in the world.

- To the church belong all those who are determined to follow Christ and proclaim him Lord and Savior.

- Local churches are "children," extensions, and a reflection of the one body of Christ, which is the "parent," the universal, the global or worldwide church.

- The many differences between local churches and denominations are not necessarily negative; they can be an enrichment.

If each denomination shares with other churches the special gifts which God has entrusted to it throughout its own history—and stays permanently self-critical, also accepting correction from the universal church— we will be able to enrich each other and grow in unity.

We are linked to the past and scattered over many places

As the church, we are part of divine salvation history. Therefore, we are united to the way of Abraham and Sarah, the pioneers of faith. And we are committed to faith and the practice of the church of the apostles. We honor the "cloud of witnesses" (Hebrews 12:1) that preceded us in church history and accompanies us now in all parts of the world.

Nevertheless, in all times, in all places, and in all cultures we exhort each other to "fix our eyes on Jesus, the author and perfecter of our faith" (Hebrews 12:2). We confess that we have often dishonored Christian fellowship. We confess that in our eager search for truth we have often lacked humility. It is difficult for us to recognize that our knowledge is limited (1 Corinthians 13:12). We have a hard time believing that we are seeing things only from our own perspective.

We forget that our personal pilgrimages, our nationalisms, and our cultural backgrounds condition our way of seeing things. We see errors and shortcomings in other cultures, in other churches, in other nations. But we are slow to recognize the sins of our own culture, our own denomination, our own nation.

Seeing clearly makes us aware of our own need for forgiveness and reconciliation.

Even though we differ from each other, we share central convictions of belief and practice

What are the things that hold the universal church together? The apostolic church, confronting the cult of Caesar, proclaimed Christ as Lord—*"Christos kyrios."* And as a secret code of identification it used the symbol of the fish, whose letters provided the initials of the confession of faith—Jesus Christ, Son of God and Savior. For many centuries and still today, the Apostles' Creed, and to a certain extent the first ecumenical councils on the Trinity and Christology, provided a common base for all Christians.

The Anabaptist Mennonite family of faith traces its origin to the radical reformers of the sixteenth century. The main merit of the radical reformation was to remind everyone that following Christ should not be imposed by governments and their reinforcements. Rather, the reformers believed that a visible and voluntary community of believers should choose to follow Christ in daily life. Their shared convictions were partly summarized in the Schleitheim Confession, 1527, and in the *Fundamentbook* by Menno Simons, 1540. They wanted to recover a vision of the church,

- determined to trust Christ for its salvation,

- determined to follow him in life, including his love for enemies, and

- determined to form a community that on earth would reflect the kingdom of God and the future heavenly city.

Almost five centuries later, after much migration and missionary outreach, descendants of these early Anabaptists include a large number of traditions, church cultures, priorities and doctrinal structures, liturgical practices, and the special expressions that come from multiple countries, languages, and cultures. These many years later, the Anabaptist-Mennonite family of faith, with the leadership of Mennonite World Conference, undertook a long and detailed process. The goal was to discover what common convictions we might now hold, despite our vastly different cultures, histories, and practices. We experienced a joyous consensus about central convictions which we all share. These convictions are explained and explored in the next seven chapters.

Study Questions

1 List actions or attitudes that are expressions of God's grace.

2 Have you observed any of these actions and attitudes in the lives of persons whom you know? If so, be ready to share a story or example.

3 Which is primarily important for Christians—what we believe or how we act? Why?

4 How do we position ourselves—as individuals, and as the body of believers—to actually function as "ambassadors of reconciliation"?

5 Is there just one body of Christ?

6 How would you describe the place which Anabaptist-related churches occupy within the body of Christ?

7 What particular blind spots do we have that keep us from behaving as Christ has called us to? What weaknesses might our sisters and brothers from elsewhere in the world point out to us, if we functioned more like a global family?

8 Do the three points in the Schleitheim Confession (summarized on page 15) represent your understanding of what is essential for the church? Is anything of significance missing?

1. We Give Glory to the Father

God is known to us as Father, Son, and Holy Spirit, the Creator who seeks to restore fallen humanity by calling a people to be faithful in fellowship, worship, service, and witness.

We know God as Father, Son, and Holy Spirit

God surpasses the capacity of our minds. So how shall we understand that Father, Son, and Holy Spirit are one? How shall we understand that the Creator of the universe took on a human body and became equal to us? That God became our brother, friend, and master, walking by our side? How can we understand that God's Spirit in Jesus Christ reveals the character of the Father to us? Even more, how are we to grasp that God dwells in us, allowing us as human beings to share divine fellowship with the Father and the Son?

St. Augustine was right when he said: *"Si compre-hendis, non est Deus."* "If you comprehend it, it's not God." God cannot be defined and escapes all our efforts to do so. We cannot imprison God with our reasoning or with our language. Nevertheless, God chose to be defined and reflected in Jesus Christ. Jesus himself claimed, "Anyone who has seen me has seen the Father" (John 14:9). And the apostle John confirmed it: "No one has ever seen God; but God, the only Son, who is at the Father's side, has made him known" (John 1:18).

The Spirit came to remind the disciples to do all that Jesus had taught and mandated. Thanks to the Spirit, we are able to pray to the Father (Romans 8:26). Thanks to the Spirit, we become able to establish Christian communication with people from other cultures (Acts 10). In both cases, the gift of the language of the Spirit makes communication possible. When the Spirit comes, the faith community emerges, with Jesus reigning in the authority given by the Father. This new community of the kingdom of the Spirit reverses all destruction caused by sin.

Christian faith in a Triune God provides hope in at least five dimensions:

- God himself as Father, Son, and Holy Spirit is God in community.

- The three persons of the Trinity provide a Christian model of relationships.

- Diversity in God and in the body of Christ is a gift and an enrichment, instead of a threat or a danger.

- The united work of Father, Son, and Holy Spirit in creation, redemption, and transformation marks the character of the kingdom of God and the holistic mission of the church.

- Thanks to the work of the Holy Spirit, we become part of divine fellowship in the holy Trinity.

We do not naturally think of parallels between the human institutions of marriage and family, and of relationships within the divine Trinity. But the Bible frequently uses relational images from human families to illuminate the Divine Being. No matter what our experiences with a human father might be, God surpasses that (Ephesians 3: 14,15). One prophet compares the mercies and the comfort of God with those of a mother (Isaiah 66:13). And elsewhere we are told that God has a covenant relationship with his people that is like the covenant between a husband and a wife. A human marriage covenant should be characterized by faithfulness and is not to be dissolved. Jesus and his church have a deep relationship much like a bride and groom, reflected in the Song of Songs of marital love.

Jesus is the perfect Son concerning love and obedience to the Father. And the Father has an extraordinary love for him (John 3:35). But the Father has the same love for any "lost son."

Relationships within a Christian family are inspired by the example of God's character (Ephesians 5:21-6:9). Furthermore, the Spirit provides unity and a bond of peace (Ephesians 4:3).

The Creator is the restorer

We believe that the earth and everything in it belongs to God and that it originated by God's creating word (Psalm 24:1,2). God is not limited by space and time or by creation. God has given beginning to the universe and will bring completion to the history of humankind.

We do not know all the scientific details, or the historic moments which were involved, as God created. But we are convinced that behind the intelligence, the beauty, the complexity, and the diversity of creation is a wise Creator. God not only gave beginning to creation, but continues to care for creation and is sustaining it with God's word and Spirit.

The powers of evil and human rebellion mistreat and cause God's creation to deteriorate, offending the Creator. But God takes the initiative to restore what

he has created. God has never abandoned the work of his hands (Psalms 138:8). Furthermore, with the sending of Jesus Christ and with the pouring out of the Spirit, God continues the work of new creation.

Those who follow Christ and know the power of the Holy Spirit have already experienced new creation in their lives. And they in turn become agents of restoration. The kingdom of God, inaugurated by Jesus Christ and promoted by the power of the Holy Spirit, lives and gives testimony to this new restored creation.

Jesus taught his disciples to pray "...your kingdom come, your will be done on earth as it is in heaven" (Matthew 6:10). The church has the joy of seeing that within its community, and even beyond, this prayer begins to become reality. Those who follow Christ get their identity and their citizenship already from heaven, the New Jerusalem (Philippians 3:20). The new, fully restored creation will be evident to all, once Christ returns in glory to judge the living and the dead and to reunite heaven and earth for eternity.

Humanity has fallen

We humans also have our beginning in God's divine purpose and design. God created us male and female, designed to live in fellowship with each other and with God, caring for creation.

We simply do not know the origin of evil. But we do perceive its destroying force in history and in our present day. Created humankind abandoned fellowship with God and even declared itself in rebellion against God. From that time on, sin and human misery have taken many forms, all caused by the breakup of fellowship between people and the Creator and the ways of life he had designed.

According to the report in Genesis, the first human couple did not trust God's good intentions for them. They wanted to be equal or even superior to God. Humankind still participates today in their act of distrust and rebellion. Their choice brought tragic consequences: they lost their dignity and began to feel ashamed; they lost their freedom and began to feel guilty; they lost their trust in God and began to feel fearful.

Humankind was created into the image of God and received the divine breath of life. This divine origin suffered fatal deterioration because of sin. The image of God, although not deleted in humankind, is often presented as a painful distortion.

We recognize that there is an extreme difference between the character of God and the character of humanity. Nevertheless, as human beings we have the possibility and the vocation to enter into a restorative relationship with our Creator. In Christ, the Creator offers to become our Father and to adopt us as children.

God is calling for a faithful people

God, who makes himself known in fellowship as Father, Son, and Holy Spirit, seeks to restore divine community through "a people." This people must be committed to God without any conditions. The Bible tells us that God found in Noah someone willing to believe and to be faithful. God saved him from the flood, together with his family and all the animals, and established a covenant with them, agreeing never again to destroy creation (Genesis 9:9-17).

With the calling of Abraham, God began the reconstruction of a people, called to be a blessing to all peoples (Genesis 12:3). The faithfulness and obedience of Abraham made him the father of faith and justice.

With Moses and the exodus from Egypt, God made himself known as the deliverer of oppressed people. God revealed his design for community living through the Ten Commandments, the celebrations, and the social instructions for the Promised Land. According to the witness of the kings and prophets of Israel, Jerusalem was called to be a light to all nations. And the covenant community was expected to be a living testimony of salvation and of a lifestyle pleasing to God.

Jesus taught his disciples that neither tradition nor religiosity itself can please God. Instead, he wanted them to understand and to do his will. With the coming of the Holy Spirit, the disciples received power to identify publicly with the way of Jesus. They started inviting all to step onto the side of Jesus and to receive the gift of the Holy Spirit and baptism. This is how the church of Jesus Christ began. The new people of God, sent to all people, testify about the new creation through the coming of the kingdom of God.

This new people must be characterized by faithfulness. Since Jesus was faithful, we ought to be faithful disciples as well. And it is our task to form new disciples, who will "obey everything that Jesus has commanded" (Matthew 28: 19, 20).

How can that be? Those who are determined to follow Christ, having received the Holy Spirit, do not automatically know everything or have all the necessary information. Jesus said they must be instructed (Matthew 28:20). When Paul talked about the important functions of church leaders, he pointed out that they all must contribute to "prepare God's people for works of service" (Ephesians 4:12). And when the apostles had to define how to be faithful to Jesus in Hebrew and in Greek culture, they called together a theological council (Acts 15). Teaching, preparation, and theological work contribute to being faithful to Jesus in different cultures and circumstances.

As God's people we want to be faithful in fellowship

The miracle of the birth of the church was the formation of a human community with extraordinary characteristics. The story of Acts tells us that in the midst of signs and wonders, the first believers were very united. They even shared their possessions so that no one would suffer need. They gathered in the temple, as well as in their homes, to praise God. Every day new persons were saved and added to their fellowship. As a community, they enjoyed the respect and favor of society. "They devoted themselves to the apostles' teaching and to the fellowship, to the breaking of bread and to prayer" (Acts 2:42-47).

The spirit of fellowship is necessary to do adequate interpretation of the Bible and to make decisions concerning the community. Fraternal fellowship is also needed to correct and to restore members who have become indifferent or rebellious in their commitment to God and to Christian ethics. Fellowship is a source of spiritual, economic, and emotional support in times of loss and suffering—death, sickness, and the powerful deceptions of life. But happy moments like weddings, anniversaries, celebrations, and achievements are also part of the fellowship of the church.

The Lord's Supper is a visible expression of fellowship with God and among members of the family of faith. When we participate, we are reconciled and united. This fellowship transcends time and space, as well as national and denominational borders. In its fellowship, the church feels united to the whole global body of Christ. In addition, those of us who belong to Anabaptist-related churches feel especially akin to that particular part of the global family.

As God's people we want to be faithful in worship

When God delivered Israel from Egypt's slavery, God liberated them so they would be able to worship him free of idolatry (Exodus 5:1). Believers during biblical times showed their adoration of God through their celebrations, sacrifices of gratitude, and in telling the mighty things God had done in history. The apostle Paul led the Ephesians in worship by retelling the story of salvation, how God had chosen and adopted them and had made them acceptable before him. In Jesus we, too, have redemption from our sin, knowledge of his will, and a foretaste of the unification of heaven and earth. The Holy Spirit is our heritage, the sign that we belong to God, and an anticipation of the glories to come (Ephesians.1:3-14). The Psalms and the book of Revelation, as well as many poems and hymns throughout the Bible, show us how to worship God.

Jesus opposed fruitless, traditional religiosity, explaining that God needs to be adored in Spirit, in truth, and with our daily lives: "These people honor me with their lips, but their hearts are far from me" (Matthew 15:8). "True worship is this: to look after orphans and widows...and to keep oneself from being polluted by the world" (James 1:27).

A worship service can include many forms of singing and praise, confession of sin and fraternal reconciliation, various readings and proclamations of God's word, testimonies, times of sharing victories and needs, as well as artistic expression. But the goal of every worship service is to renew our covenant with God and with the church by recommitting our lives as believers to the service of God (Romans 12:1-2).

As God's people we want to be faithful in service

When Jesus wanted to explain to his disciples the mission that brought him to earth, he invited them to a banquet and he washed their feet. With this example, he wanted us to know that service is the most excellent divine characteristic. It stands in sharp contrast to the attitude of the powerful of this world: "You know that the rulers of the Gentiles lorded over them....Not so with you. Instead, whoever wants to become great among you, must be your servant...just as the Son of Man did not come to be served, but to serve, and to give his life as a ransom for many" (Matthew 20:25-28).

The first church elected deacons very early on. They needed them to lead the community in the attitude and practice of service. The deacons had to be full of the Holy Spirit and to be persons with good reputations. Some of them later became evangelists. They had to resolve interethnic conflicts, look after justice, and assure that the needy would be cared for adequately. In times of famine, the apostle Paul took a large money offering from the young missionary churches to the impoverished mother church of Jerusalem. And he instructed all believers: "Let us not become weary in doing good....Let us do good to all people, especially to those who belong to the family of believers" (Galatians 6:9-10).

The service of the church is directed towards the community within—and also to the outside community. The church offers public service, and it has political impact. It includes all human needs: the emo-

tional dimension, the spiritual, the economic, health, education, moments of violence, natural disaster and war, prison and injustice. Christian service, as well as evangelism, edification, fellowship, and theological work, must move from all nations to all nations. It is not uni-directional. This is so because the church is present in every *local* and particular congregation, as well as in the *global* body of Christ.

As God's people we want to be faithful in witness

In the language of the Bible, the same word is used for being a witness and for being a martyr. A witness is one with faith who gives voice to the things s/he has seen and heard. A martyr is willing to give his or her life in order to endorse his or her testimony. When the Holy Spirit came, Jesus promised his timid disciples that they would be his witnesses in Judea, Samaria, and to the end of the world (Acts 1:8). The Holy Spirit followed up the witness of the disciples, doing signs and wonders and convincing people. And Jesus himself is God's most excellent and faithful witness (Revelation 1:5).

The church witnesses by its living presence. Jesus assigned his disciples the function of being salt and light in the earth and throughout the entire world. He made clear that the presence of the disciples must have a transforming impact on their social environment: "A new commandment I give you: Love one another, as I have loved you....All people will know that you are my disciples, if you love one another" (John 13:34-35). This is the reason why the life and the testimony of the church deserves our highest attention. Not only individual missionaries, but also entire faith communities, should migrate to areas where there is not a Christian witness to become a means of hope and evangelism.

The church witnesses through evangelistic proclamation. It would be naïve to believe that the Christian witness does not need verbal proclamation and explanation. The deacon and evangelist Philip met a high Ethiopian official reading the Bible. He asked, "'Do you understand, what you are reading?' He said, 'How can I, unless someone explains it to me?'.... Then Philip began with that very passage of Scripture and told him the good news about Jesus" (Acts 8:30-35). Francis of Assisi said, "Witness always, and when necessary, use your mouth."

The church witnesses through prophetic announcement and denouncement. Jesus was a king and a priest, but he also was a prophet. In the same way, his church has a prophetic and a public role to announce and denounce. Martin Luther King, Jr. and Dietrich Bonhoeffer have rightly been considered prophets of the twentieth century because they denounced racism and discrimination, and they paid with their lives.

When the church denounces violence and injustice and is unwilling to take up arms against any enemy, it gives testimony to the character and love of Jesus Christ. When the church announces better forms of shared human living, of conflict resolution, of care for creation and stewardship of resources, it witnesses to the heavenly city and to the kingdom of God begun on earth. When the church chooses not to participate in corruption, idolatry, hate, despising, discrimination, and materialism, it publicly calls for repentance from all forms of sin.

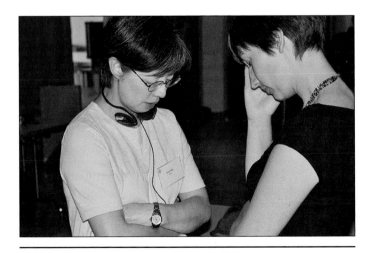

Study Questions

1 What is "the gift of the language of the Spirit" in your experience?

2 What do you think of the idea that God as Father, Son, and Holy Spirit is "God in community"?

3 In what ways do those three persons of the Trinity "provide a Christian model of relationships" for you?

4 In what ways do you observe God continuing to care for and sustain creation?

5 How have you seen God the creator undoing shame, guilt, and fear, the three consequences of Adam's and Eve's behavior, still painfully present today?

6 Why has God chosen to work not just with individuals, but with "a people"? Why is a covenant community so vital?

7 What all should "fellowship" include beyond having a good time together?

8 Explore the ways in which the Lord's Supper is both a concrete, local event, while at the same time it allows those who are participating to transcend time and space.

9 Consider your congregation's worship services. In what ways do they lead participants toward renewing their personal covenants with God and the church? In what ways do they contribute to participants committing themselves to God's service?

10 How does the church attend both to the needs of its neighborhood and the general society, as well as to its own community of believers?

11 How can we bring back together the call to serve and the call to proclaim, as the deacons in the first church did?

12 How will your congregation, and your national church, position itself to receive what it needs from other congregations and churches within the global family of faith?

13 Name specific ways in which your congregation is being a faithful witness at this time.

2. We Give Glory to the Son

Jesus is the Son of God. Through his life and teachings, his cross and resurrection, he showed us how to be faithful disciples, he redeemed the world, and offers eternal life.

Jesus shows us who God is

Jesus was born more than 2,000 years ago to a young Jewish woman. When she understood God's plan, she composed a beautiful poem of worship. She claimed that the son to whom she would give birth was the Messiah the people of Israel were waiting for. When the baby was born, he received the name "Jesus," which means "God helps." And the name "Christ" means "Messiah," which in the Hebrew language is the same as the title, "the anointed of God."

Christ usually referred to himself as the "Son of Man." When he began to gather disciples and to explain to them the new time which God was bringing about, he said, "For the Son of Man came to seek and save what was lost" (Luke 19:10). His birth and growing up, his social life and his physical necessities, his joys and his sufferings, his struggle with temptations and his search for God's presence—all of this shows us that he was entirely human. That is why those who lived with him said, "He was made like us in every way" (Hebrews 2:17).

When the disciples wrote the Gospels, they did it with the full conviction that Jesus was the Son of God. They had heard of his wondrous birth and the divine wisdom which he showed from his teenage years on, even impressing the learned ones of those times. Some of his followers were present at his baptism when the Holy Spirit visibly came upon Jesus. They had seen many miracles and healings, not explainable by human means. When they were together with him on Mount Tabor, they had a vision of him in divine fellowship with Moses and the prophet Elijah.

At one time the crowd of people was divided about him. Jesus asked his disciples, "'But what about you?.... Who do you say I am?' Simon Peter answered, 'You are the Christ, the Son of the living God'" (Matthew 16:15-16). And when it became dangerous to follow Christ, he offered that they could leave him. But they answered, "'Lord, to whom shall we go? You have the words of eternal life. We believe and know that you are the Holy One of God'" (John 6:68-69).

The Christian community of faith proclaims that Christ was an extraordinary and unique person. He was 100% God and 100% human. He had an entirely divine origin and showed us the heart and character of God. He had an entirely human origin and showed us the human character which God wants to restore in us.

We are convinced that Christian faith has an extraordinary element which we have not found in other beliefs. God becomes human so that we can know God. God becomes human, not leaving us alone, but walking by our side and offering us love. Christ helps us to correct wrong ideas we might have concerning God. He said, "'I and the Father are one'" (John 10:30). "'And whoever sees me, sees the Father'" (John 14:9). It is to Jesus that we must look, if we want to know who God is and what God is up to.

The life of Jesus is our model

Albert Schweitzer (1875-1965) was a young and very successful student of theology at a university in Strasbourg, France. He also had become famous as an organist and expert in the sacred music of Bach. The concerts which he played on the exclusive Silberman organs attracted European high society.

After he turned 30, he told of hearing the voice of Jesus with a calling to follow him in life. He decided to study medicine and dedicate the rest of his life to the needy population of Gabon, Africa. His hospital in Lambarene speaks not only about authentic Christian humanism. It also gives testimony to the fact that following Christ in life brings great blessing to those marginalized by society.

Jesus is the way. He also is the truth and the life. None of comes to God unless we walk this way, learn this truth, and have part in this life (John 14:6). Paul speaks of the importance of this reality when he points out that Christ in us is the hope of glory (Colossians 1:27). But it also works the other way around.

Living in Christ delivers us from sin and death: "...the law of the Spirit of living in Christ set me free from the law of sin and death" (Romans 8:2).

Jesus is the healer (Exodus 15:26). Jesus had only about three years of public ministry. Nevertheless, he dedicated a large amount of his time and energy to the sick. At that time, the most marginalized in society were those suffering from leprosy. Jesus identified with them. The demon-possessed suffered special oppression from the devil and the powers of evil. Jesus set them free. Many people broken in heart and body, depressed and discouraged, young and old came to him. They learned to know him as the divine healer.

Jesus is the teacher. Large crowds of people came to hear his teachings. They gave him the Hebrew title, Rabbi. Jesus taught by the way he lived, but also with other methods, especially the parables. Any place was good to teach: a hill, a boat, the temple, the synagogue, banquets, and personal encounters. At

the end of the Sermon on the Mount we read, "When Jesus had finished saying these things, the crowds were amazed at his teaching, because he taught as one who had authority, and not as their teachers of the law" (Matthew 7:28-29).

Jesus is the good shepherd (John 10:11). As such, he gave leadership and protection to the group of his disciples. But he also tried to gather the scattered and lost sheep of the people of Israel who suffered under oppression by the Roman Empire (Matthew 9:36). He invited all the "weary and burdened" to find "rest' with the good shepherd (Matthew 11:28). He defined the salvation that he brought in relational terms: "My sheep listen to my voice; I know them, and they follow me. I give them eternal life, and they shall never perish; no one can snatch them out of my hand" (John 10:27-28).

Jesus is our friend. The religious elite of his time accused Jesus of being a friend of "tax collectors and sinners" (Luke 7:34). When his friend Lazarus died, Jesus wept. He told his disciples, "Greater love has no one than this, that one lay down his life for his friends....I no longer call you servants....Instead, I have called you friends, for everything that I learned from my Father I have made known to you" (John 15:13-15).

The teaching of Jesus gives us orientation

Jesus began his ministry of teaching by saying that the messianic promises of the Old Testament are fulfilled in him (Luke 4:21). He became the best teacher of the history, the law, the prophets, and the wisdom of the people of God.

Jesus reverses values. The disciples got a new ethic and learned a new political platform while hearing the beatitudes and the Sermon on the Mount (Matthew 5-7). Jesus declared blessed the "poor in spirit, those who mourn and are meek, those who hunger for righteousness, the merciful and pure in heart, the peacemakers and those persecuted because of righteousness, and those falsely insulted through lies because of him" (Matthew 5:3-11).

Jesus brings a new liturgy. Among the most radical teachings of Jesus were his instructions concerning prayer and worship. He recommended that his disciples avoid long prayers, as well as deeds of charity made public. He taught helping one's neighbor without calling attention to it, and praying to God in private. For praying together, he gave them the Lord's Prayer, which in a brief manner shows how to pray for the coming of the kingdom and how to pray for personal and spiritual needs (Matthew 6:1-34).

Jesus proclaims the ethic of love. He prohibited his disciples from loving money and making idols of material goods. He exhorted them to love the dispossessed and marginalized in the same way as they loved their close friends. And in all cases, he required overcoming evil by good, renouncing vengeance, and avoiding hostility that invades the heart. He taught his followers to absorb the hate of the world by meekness. "But I tell you: Love your enemies, bless those who curse you, do good to those who hate you, and pray

for those who persecute you, that you may be children of your Father in heaven" (Matthew 5:44-45).

Jesus teaches us to prepare ourselves for the future. When Jesus left his disciples to be taken to heaven, he commanded them to work in the power of the Holy Spirit until he would return in glory (Luke 19:13). Living with an orientation towards the future, on one hand, means "to accumulate treasures in heaven" and to have one's heart immersed in the culture coming from there (Matthew 6:19-21). But it also means to be prepared for the great final judgment, when every human being will be responsible for the things s/he did or did not do in life (Matthew 25:31-46).

The death of Jesus makes us free

Jesus' death on the cross teaches us how to love. The apostle Paul had reasons enough to be proud and to boast about himself. But he said emphatically that he just wanted to boast in the cross of Christ (Galatians 6:14). Those of us following Christ today affirm the same, because we know the power and the wisdom of the cross.

The cross is the highest expression of love. With his open arms, the Crucified not only embraced his loved ones, but also his enemies and the whole world. He expressed love towards religious and political leaders, who in a cynical way executed him. He loved fanatic egoists, brutal soldiers, and a cruel crowd. He offered his love to cowardly disciples and desperate women: "...because God's love has been poured out into our hearts...at just the right time, when we were still powerless, Christ died for the ungodly" (Romans 5:5-6). God's love shown on the cross restores us into a family.

Christ's death on the cross brings healing. Our own rebellions, our self-centeredness, the destructive forces of the powers of evil, our many personal and structural sins, the whole creation distanced from God—all of that causes wounds and sufferings. But the cross of Christ has a healing power; it has a reconciling power. Through his wounds we have been healed (Isaiah 53:5).

Christ's death on the cross heals through reconciliation: "But now in Christ Jesus you who once were far away have been brought near through the blood of Christ" (Ephesians 2:13). Through the cross, God reconciles "in this one body both of them, putting death to their hostility" (Ephesians 2:16). The cross of Christ functions like a *hospital*.

Christ's death on the cross constitutes a victory. The Bible tells us that beginning with Adam, the first

man, we have been invaded and enslaved by the powers of evil. Our own strength and our sense of responsibility are not enough to resist sin and do good. But Christ on the cross said, "It is finished" (John 19:30). We believe that from that moment on, he achieved a cosmic victory, and he makes us part of this victory. "And having disarmed the powers and authorities, he made a public spectacle of them, triumphing over them by the cross" (Colossians 2:15). That is why we shall not have fear: "In this world you will have trouble. But take heart! I have overcome the world" (John 16:33). What seemed to be a defeat at the cross has become the symbol of a won battle.

Christ's death on the cross restores our dignity. The Bible tells us that sin brings with it a culture of death. And those "enslaved by sin" commit shameful things in the light of divine justice. But thanks to the cross, we left "the slavery of impurity and ever increasing wickedness...things you are now ashamed of." God restores us to become "servants" of God and gives us "sanctification." "For the wages of sin is death, but the gift of God is eternal life in Christ Jesus, our Lord" (Romans 6:15-23). The cross makes possible a life of dignity that honors God and this new creation.

Christ's death on the cross sets us free from prison. Being imprisoned by sin does not just rob our dignity. It also makes us guilty before God and fills us with feelings of guilt. For the bad things we do are our own responsibilities. To be guilty before God deserves divine condemnation. And feelings of guilt depress us. But the cross of Christ sets us free because it cancels our guilt. "When you were dead in your sins...God made you alive with Christ. God forgave us all our sins, having canceled the written code, with its regulations, that was against us and that stood opposed to us; he took it away, nailing it to the cross" (Colossians 2:13-14). Thanks to the cross, we abandon prison and recover as free human beings.

The resurrection of Jesus gives us hope

In my country, Paraguay, we have a very successful and famous journalist. Because of his Jewish background and his opposition to the totalitarian military government, he suffered mistreatment and persecution. He declares himself to be a great admirer of Jesus. The life and the teachings of Christ express for him a profound and noble humanism worthy to be imitated. But the biblical report of the resurrection does not make sense to him at all.

Christ's tomb was empty. The crucified was resurrected. With the death of Christ, his followers were profoundly confused, disappointed, frustrated, and frightened. They took it for granted that Christ's death was the end of the story. We can imagine the surprise, the unbelief, but also the joy and the euphoria, when the first witnesses on Easter morning discovered that the tomb was empty. And when they had several encounters with the resurrected, who greeted them with peace and took away their fear, they began to understand the whole dimension of Christ the Messiah. They realized that the promised kingdom had begun, because death had been defeated by the resurrection of Christ.

The story of Jesus goes on. The book of Acts continues the story of the risen Jesus. Through his disciples, acting in the power of the Holy Spirit, the good news of the risen Jesus, the Messiah of the world, began to move through the Roman Empire. And in many places Christian churches emerged, the visible body of the risen Christ.

We have been resurrected with Christ. With the resurrection of Christ, God started the restoration of the world in a visible way. This restoration began in a hidden and invisible way, first in the minds and the hearts of Christ's followers. They formed a visible new community of believers who "walked in the resurrection." They experienced a quality of new spiritual life like the resurrected Christ had. The kingdom of God works like mustard seed: small genetics—large consequences.

Death is displaced by life. The Bible tells us that the enemy of God comes to "rob, kill and destroy" (John 10:8-10). All that is wrong in the present creation—the structures of sin, the harmful elements in human cultures—has its origin and strength in the thoughts and hearts of human beings. And precisely there, new life begins. Jesus brings abundant life. When Adam and Eve chose the wrong way, humankind was overcome by cultures of death. But through Christ, resurrection and life has come (Romans 5:12-19).

Victorino was a street boy in Asunción who ended up in the national prison, Tacumbú. Félix Duarte Dupont, himself a former inmate, is now a pastor and leader of a rehabilitation program in the Mennonite church, Libertad, within that same prison. During a church service Felix told the story of how a street boy shot him through his foot while trying to rob his cell phone. And then Victorino began vaguely to remember that when he was on drugs, he shot a guy who was running in the park. The next day the paper reported that the victim was a priest or a pastor. Victorino began to remember more. A young boy was with the priest and tried to defend him. Victorino had aimed his pistol three times at the boy's face and pulled the trigger. But three times no shot came out. Later that evening, he checked what had happened. He saw the three bullets, each with the mark of the trigger. There was no visible reason that they hadn't exploded.

As time passed in prison, Victorino became convinced that the guy he had been shooting at was the prison pastor, Félix, and that the young guy whom his pistol had failed to shoot was Marcelo, the son of the pastor. Three months later, the three appeared on a TV show, telling how Christ had changed Victorino's "culture of death" toward a "culture of life," and how God's grace had been transforming violence into love in the hearts of all three.

New creation is possible, thanks to the resurrection. A new creation of God traces its beginning to the resurrection of Christ. New creation is powerfully promoted by the Holy Spirit of God and the church of the risen Christ. But there is much more to come in a future moment, when God once more will intervene visibly in human history. Then God will fully fulfill the promise: "I am making everything new" (Revelation 21:5). All of creation will be absorbed and transformed into the new creation.

The faithfulness of Jesus enables us to be faithful

Salvation means a relationship of faithfulness with Jesus. No, we never will be like Jesus. He was divine;

we are human. But because he became human, he fully understands our temptations and limitations. Nevertheless, he invites us to walk with him and to learn from his faithfulness. "Your attitude should be the same as that of Christ Jesus....he made himself nothing, taking the very nature of a servant...and became obedient to death" (Philippians 2:5-8).

We want to be faithful to the way of Jesus. And so we want to be faithful to his teachings. We want to be faithful to his example of living. We want to be faithful to the priorities and values which Jesus lived and taught. We want to faithfully love our friends and enemies, as Jesus did in life and on the cross. We want to rejoice as we participate in the new life of his resurrection.

In the Bible, the concepts of faith, faithfulness, and righteousness are intimately linked. Because Jesus was faithful, we have become righteous. To

have faith means to be faithful. The faithfulness of Jesus brought forth our justification before God. But this justice which we received is a lot more than an act of divine declaration. It brings with it participation in the faithfulness and life of justice which Jesus himself practiced and wants to make possible in us. Think of it as a criminal who needs Christ, and after believing in Christ becomes a lawful and righteous person. "Therefore, since we have been justified through faith [or faithfulness], we have peace with God through our Lord Jesus Christ" (Romans 5:1). This passage makes it clear that if we have faith we will be faithful.

The way of Jesus redeems the world

Christ is the king of all. This is the title which the Bible gives him (Revelation 1:5). It means that all moral and spiritual authority is given to him. With his project of transformation, he seeks to reach the whole world. It is obvious that not all human beings recognize Christ as king. But we are convinced and believe that this will change at a certain moment in the future.

Christ is the priest for all (Hebrews 4:14-15). The salvation Christ brings is for the whole world. The function of the priest was to bring about reconciliation: "But if anybody does sin, we have one who speaks to the Father in our defense—Jesus Christ the Righteous One. He is the atoning sacrifice for our sins, and not only for ours, but also for the sins of the whole world" (1 John 2:1-2). God's reconciliation is for all of humanity.

Christ is the prophet for all. The teachings of Christ are valid for the whole world (Matthew 28:19-20). A prophet makes known the will of God and calls believers to live it. As such he is a faithful witness of God.

Jesus makes us participants in his titles and declares us to be a people of kings, priests, and prophets who belong to God (1 Peter 2:9). To be a prophet means to declare the will of God in specific situations. To be a priest means to be an instrument who helps people relate to God. To belong to a family of kings speaks of dignity and a high calling which we receive when we belong to God's family.

Christ is the judge of all (Acts 10:42). The Bible tells us that there will be final judgment in the future, when all of us human beings will be accountable before our Creator and Lord. God considers us capable of assuming responsibility for our deeds and our choices. The last judgment has two practical implications: On the one hand, we are called not to judge others, but to leave judgment to God (Matthew 7:1). On the other hand, it also means that we are called to care and to work for just conditions within the community of believers as well as in society in general. We are called to help resolve conflicts according to the ethic and Spirit of Jesus (1 Corinthians 6:1-7).

Christ is the good shepherd for the whole world (John 10:11). His love is directed to all of humanity, especially to the most lost and needy. A pastor gives protection, nurtures, heals, and leads. Most of all, s/he seeks to keep the flock united. Jesus wants the whole flock of his followers to be in unity (John 10:16). Even

more, he seeks to attract the whole of humanity to his love and way of living (John 12:32).

Whoever is united to Jesus has eternal life

How shall we imagine eternal life? In our experience, nothing is eternal. Our whole perception is bound to the realities of space and time. When the Bible talks about eternal life, it wants to open our minds toward a reality beyond space and time. Eternal life has to do with a divine dimension that our natural senses do not perceive. This means at least five things:

- Eternity begins here and now. Eternal life does not begin after death. It is given by God in the moment when someone decides to proclaim

Christ as Lord and Savior and to surrender his/ her life unconditionally. It is very clear: "Whoever believes in the Son has eternal life" (John 3:36).

- Eternal life means belonging to the new age of the kingdom of God. When Christ came, even more so when he poured out his Spirit, the new times began. The church has eternal life because the eternal Christ is in its midst already. It already wants to do God's will on earth as in heaven. It already lives a new culture, which can be called the culture of the body of Christ. We have heard a lot about New Age philosophy and ideology. We Christians should proactively and publicly hold that the "New Age" is a Christian idea. Since the coming of Christ, the "New Age" has come. Wherever Christ enters and is present in individual lives, families, communities, and cultures, things start to change because a "New Age" has become reality.

- Eternal life means that death has been overcome. Eternal life means that death cannot cause real changes anymore. Of course, with death, one time period ends and another reality begins. Of course, death destroys our bodies. But the same eternal life, which began in our lives with the resurrection of Christ, becomes complete fulfillment, clarity, and joy after death.

- Eternal life is that which the Holy Spirit causes in our hearts and in our communities. Who guarantees us the reality of eternal life? Who is capable of bringing heaven to earth? Who is

capable of transforming earth into heaven? It is the Holy Spirit, the presence of the Triune God in our hearts and in our churches. And this Spirit has been poured out on "all people" (Acts 2:17).

• Eternal life means freedom forever from sin and condemnation. There is a special hope that we followers of Christ hold with complete assurance—the security that nothing can separate us from God's love (Romans 8:18-39)—not the present, not the future, not death, not our own weakness. Those who choose to live without God cannot expect to enjoy God's presence in eternity. But those who know Christ and have followed him in life will have no condemnation. When time is no more, they will still be in divine fellowship.

Study Questions

1 Imagine that someone asked you, "Who do you say Jesus is?" Answer as clearly and as truthfully as you can.

2 In what way(s) has Jesus been one of the following in your life—healer, the "way," teacher, the "truth," good shepherd, the "life," friend.

3 In what way(s) has Jesus been one of those for your congregation?

4 How do your congregation's worship services orient your day-to-day life toward Jesus? What practices or elements are especially helpful? What should be strengthened?

5 Where is the overlap between your life and the Sermon on the Mount?

6 What connection do you see between Christ dying on a cross—and healing? Between Christ dying on a cross—and reconciliation? Between Christ dying on a cross—and your dignity?

7 In what ways have you been "resurrected with Christ"?

8 How does your congregation "walk in the resurrection"?

9 Do you agree that if one of the following characteristics is present in your life, the other two are also: "faith," "faithfulness," and "righteousness"? Explain.

10 How does your faith community participate in Jesus' titles and functions as "kings," "priests," and "prophets"? Be specific.

11 What are some of the concrete characteristics of the church's "new culture," which it experiences because it has already begun its eternal life in Christ?

3. We Give Glory to the Holy Spirit

As a church, we are a community of those whom God's Spirit calls to turn from sin, acknowledge Jesus Christ as Lord, receive baptism upon confession of faith, and follow Christ in life.

When the Holy Spirit came, the church was born as a community of believers

The church cannot live without the Holy Spirit. Today, many churches seem to go on, thanks to their traditions, their schedules, their rites, and their church calendars, which remind them of the important Christian festivities. Someone has alerted us to a serious reality: "If the Holy Spirit would be removed from earth, many churches might not even notice it." Tragic if true, because the church without the Holy Spirit is nothing. It would be a merely human phenomenon of sociology of religion or of religious cultural tradition.

The Holy Spirit is the dynamic presence of God. We have said that the Trinity is a mystery inaccessible to our minds, and we accept the fact that this is so. Jesus himself promised his permanent presence to his disciples. He was referring to the power of the Holy Spirit which they would receive. Our daily experience confirms to us that we are weak and incapable of responding in a satisfying manner to divine expectations. It is here where the Holy Spirit intervenes. Paul said to Timothy: "For God did not give us a spirit of timidity, but a spirit of power, of love and of self-discipline" (2 Timothy 1:7). And for the church in Ephesus it was his prayer that God "may strengthen you with power through his Spirit in your inner being" (Ephesians 3:16).

The Holy Spirit is the critical presence of God. The origin of the words "crisis" and "critique" has to do with judgment and with decisions. Through the church, the Holy Spirit wants to do more than promote things that please God. It also wants to lay bare and judge all which opposes God's kingdom and God's justice. The Holy Spirit, and with it also the church, exercises a critical function in the world. Wherever the light shines, darkness is defeated. Wherever justice is manifest, injustice is made evident.

We live in the time of the church and the Holy Spirit. This, God the Lord of history, has determined. Beyond political and economic powers, beyond forces of globalization, there is reality seen from God's perspective. It is the time of the church in the power of the Holy Spirit. God has placed the whole redeeming

project on behalf of humanity into the hands of the church. Of course, the church has often been unfaithful. But God has chosen to bring his redeeming message to the whole world, and to make Christ visible to those that do not know him, through the church. The church is the salt of the earth and the light of the world, because Christ himself is present in the church through the dynamic and critical presence of the Holy Spirit.

The church is made up of believers. Believers are those who have placed their faith unconditionally in Jesus Christ. No, the church is not those special buildings that we might first think of. Neither is it the powerful national and worldwide organizations that we might associate with the church. We believe that the church is not basically made up of sacraments and rituals, traditions, structures, or bylaws.

The church is living beings. The church is those people who have experienced the transforming power of the Holy Spirit. The Bible refers to this experience as "baptism with the Holy Spirit" and "the fullness of the Holy Spirit" (Matthew 3:11; Ephesians 1:13; Ephesians 4:23; Ephesians 4:30; Ephesians 5:18). This experience involves at least four moments: turning away from sin, submitting to the lordship of Christ, communicating the confession of faith through baptism, and deciding to follow Christ in life.

Wherever the Holy Spirit works, people turn away from sin

Sin is the great tragedy of humankind. Most of the shortcomings in our society are due to human sin. Sin is all that is incompatible with the character and the will of God. We become vulnerable to sin whenever we distance ourselves from communion with God. Sin also has to do with goals and directions. We sin when we go in wrong directions and when we do not share the goals which the Creator has for our lives. There are sins of action and omission, doing bad things and not doing good things.

The Bible tells us about the possibility of "putting off our old selves." Christ did not just bring the new times of the kingdom of God. God also brought the possibility of personal renewal. The Bible talks about this reality in creation language: "...what counts is a new creation" (Galatians 6:15). But there is no new creation without "putting off," like there is no butterfly without leaving the cocoon. "You were taught, with regard to your former way of life, to put off your old self, which is being corrupted by its deceitful desires" (Ephesians 4:22). A "yes" to Christ also requires a "no" to non-Christian attitudes.

The Bible also tells us about the possibility of "putting on a new self." The kingdom of God and God's righteousness is being brought forward by "new" human beings, who already have experienced new creation: "...to be made new in the attitude of your minds; and to put on the new self, created to be like God in true righteousness and holiness" (Ephesians 4:23-24). Holiness is all that which is intimately linked to God and which reflects God's being.

Looking at Jesus is the best way to turn away from sin. When I learned to ride a bicycle, I found that the best way of keeping my balance and staying on the path was to look ahead to the goal I wanted to reach. To abandon sin becomes possible when a new passion fills our souls. Paul tells us that the only way he could forget his past errors was by concentrating on Christ's project, committing himself totally to him (Philippians 3:12). The letter of Hebrews tells us that we are not alone in our struggle against sin and our commitment to the cause of Christ. We are accompanied by a "great cloud of witnesses" who also "fixed their eyes on Jesus" (Hebrews 12:1-2).

Jesus said that sin might contaminate the church. Sin has a destructive power in the church and in society in general. It would be an error to oppose sin by violence. It is an error to reject persons that struggle with sin and fail. Jesus came precisely for them. But it is necessary to confront sin with determination.

Outside of the church we do it with prophetic denouncement and with a good example. Within the church Jesus tells us to use fraternal admonishment. This must begin in a private setting so that our companion in faith is not publicly shamed. If the person shows no "turning away from sin," it becomes necessary to address the situation in front of witnesses, and, in a last attempt, in front of the congregation of believers.

Jesus gives a special promise of his presence to those who seek to correct each other and to help each other to turn away from sin (Matthew 18:15-20). Of course, there is the danger of legalism with such efforts. There is also the danger of church abuse in discipline. But the church that fails to distance itself from sin loses credibility, respect, and authority.

Wherever the Holy Spirit convinces, people acknowledge Jesus Christ as Lord

Jesus is the Lord of the kingdom of God. If someone becomes part of the family of faith through the power of the Holy Spirit, s/he also becomes part of the church and the kingdom of God, because s/he acknowledges a new lordship in life. Christian freedom consists precisely in having a new lord, who at the same time is brother and friend. For the same reason, the church does not accept any other headship except Christ. For the same reason, the people of God do not recognize leadership that does not grow out of full identification with Christ. For the same reason, the kingdom of God receives its character from the king himself, Christ Jesus the Lord.

Prior to World War II, when the nation of Germany prepared itself to be led by just one "Führer," there was a real danger that human and political leadership would be given the honors that belong only to Jesus Christ. So the "Confessing Church," under the leadership of Swiss theologian Karl Barth, launched a brave public statement known as the "Barmen Declaration." Its opening paragraph states, "The church does not recognize any other lordship than the lordship of Jesus Christ."

How does the history of God's kingdom relate to the history of the world? Which is the real story—the "secular" history or the "sacred" history? The answer to this question depends on our perspective. The Bible tells us that "those who are unspiritual do not receive the gifts of God's spirit" (1 Corinthians 2:14). Therefore, without the Holy Spirit, it is difficult for us to perceive the history of the kingdom of God in the midst of the history of humankind.

From God's perspective there is just one history. For God there is no separation between the secular and the sacred. We tend to see a Sunday worship service as something "sacred" and our everyday, during-the-week job reality as something "secular." This is a separation that arises from human unbelief. The truth is that everything belongs under the lordship of Christ. With his incarnation, Jesus entered visibly into human history. His life and death, his resurrection and ascension, but also the church through the power of the Holy Spirit and Christ's return in glory, are realities that impact human history.

When we talk about God's kingdom we distinguish it from other kingdoms. Can it be that the kingdom of God will fuse completely with human reality and human history? Yes and no. It is true that Christ's lordship and God's kingdom want to be totally incarnated in human reality. It is true that the gospel has a transforming power for all areas of human existence and human culture. Nothing is excluded. But God's kingdom is different because it is not oriented around self-centeredness and hostilities. Instead, it is expressed in the priorities and values which Jesus himself brought. When the kingdom of God entered the life of Zaccheus, he continued to be the little guy known about his town, but it soon became evident that a new rule of values and priorities was orienting his life.

When we talk about kingdom, we are talking about questions of power. There are no changes without power. But there is legitimate and illegitimate power. Illegitimate power is nurtured by egoism and leads to injustice. Legitimate power is compatible with the character of God and the life of Jesus. This is the power given by the Holy Spirit. The followers of Christ should not search for a different kind of power.

Whoever evokes the kingdom of God strives for change. Most of humanity longs for change. Many fear that our changing times do not bring changes for the good. The good news of the gospel is that changes for good are possible. This is confirmed by those who resolve to turn away from sin. In any place, in any community, in any culture where Christ is proclaimed Lord, changes for the good will become visible.

Wherever the Holy Spirit takes hold of human life, people confess their faith through baptism

Adult water baptism illustrates the baptism of the Holy Spirit. We do not believe that the rite of baptism in itself has saving strength. But we believe it is a practice that powerfully communicates a message. The Anabaptist church in its beginning was persecuted severely because its practice of baptism redefined the concept of salvation, the concept of the church, and the concept of Christian life. When the Bible speaks of the baptism of the Holy Spirit, it sums up this whole message well. Water baptism expresses and communicates this event publicly.

Adult water baptism illustrates death and resurrection with Christ. When the Holy Spirit works in the lives of individuals, something dies and something rises: "We were therefore buried with Christ through baptism into death in order that, just as Christ was raised from the dead through the glory of the Father, we too may live a new life" (Romans 6:4).

Adult water baptism illustrates the washing of all sins. In many hot countries, baths and washings are especially important because of dust and sweat. But in addition to those reasons, the people of Israel received special instructions about purity and cleansings so that they could stand in God's presence. In the Bible, sin is considered something which makes us dirty and unpleasant before God and our neighbors. The act of baptism expresses the purifying work that the Holy Spirit produces as a result of Christ's redemptive action.

Adult water baptism illustrates being incorporated into the community of Christ's body. Some churches consider baptism and membership in a local church to be two different things. They explain that with baptism we enter into the "invisible" church. But we believe that the church should always be visible. We believe that through the gift of the Holy Spirit, illustrated and expressed in baptism, we become part of the global *and also* the local church: "For we were all baptized by one Spirit into one body—whether Jews or Greeks, slave or free" (1 Corinthians 12:13).

Adult water baptism illustrates a public covenant. We have talked about God's covenant with Noah, Abraham, and the people of Israel. We have seen that in Jesus, God restored a people of covenant in the New Testament. The personal and public way to demonstrate a covenant commitment with God and with the church is expressed in baptism. It is a covenant to follow Christ in life, together with the community of believers.

Whoever belongs to the church of the Holy Spirit wants to follow Christ in life

What would Jesus do? What would Jesus think? What would Jesus say? These questions have had a profound impact on the lives of great Christian innovators. We have already seen that Albert Schweitzer decided to follow Christ through medical service. Dietrich Bonhoeffer and Martin Niemöller, asking themselves what Jesus would do, strongly opposed the anti-Christian ideology of the Nazi regime. Throughout history, these questions have oriented women and men to live lives that make a difference in their times.

Where does this wish to follow Christ in life come from? It is definitely the work of the Holy Spirit. "But the Counselor, the Holy Spirit,...will teach you all things and will remind you of everything I have said to you" (John 14:26). This is what Jesus promised. And Paul added: "But we have the mind of Christ" (1 Corinthians 2:16). And he also exhorted us, "Your attitude should be the same as that of Christ Jesus" (Philippians 2:5).

To be able to follow Christ in life is a gift of God. We do not achieve it with our own efforts. In fact, the opposite is true. Many times we fail and dishonor the way of the Lord. But the grace of God, given to us through the presence of the Holy Spirit, does not only forgive our failures, but also strengthens us and makes us able to follow Christ in life.

Anyone—without exception—can choose to follow Christ. There is no discrimination between men and women, between different groups, or between social classes. Following Christ overcomes discrimination. The Holy Spirit gives us the impetus to follow Christ into cross-cultural mission. The apostle Peter learned this when Jesus sent him to the house of Cornelius, a Roman military man. The Holy Spirit did not allow him to call impure what God had made pure. And when Cornelius received the Holy Spirit, Peter said, "I now realize how true it is that God does not show favoritism but accepts anyone from every nation who fears him and does what is right" (Acts 10:34-35).

Living with Christ is valid not only in life, but also in death. Or maybe it is more true to say that if in life we walked with Jesus, in the hour of our death he walks with us.

Paul concluded, "So, whether we live or die, we belong to the Lord" (Romans 14:8). Eternal life is defined simply as "...we will be with the Lord forever" (1 Thessalonians 4:17).

Study Questions

1. Do you believe the church that you are part of is well equipped enough to carry out God's "whole redeeming project" for humanity? What evidence do you see or experience?

2. What evidence is there that the church is a greater force than the powers of politics, economics, and globalization, as Alfred claims on pages 56-57?

3 How can you personally, as well as your congregation, experience more of the Holy Spirit's shaping and power?

4 How, practically, do humans and God work together at the project of "putting off our old selves" and "putting on new selves"?

5 In what ways can we access the strength that comes from being surrounded by a "great cloud of witnesses"?

6 How can the church admonish its own, and help each other to turn away from sin, without making a situation worse?

7 Do mature Christians see all within their lives as "sacred," no longer differentiating between the "secular" and the "sacred"?

8 Power is often a negative word for Christians belonging to Anabaptist-related churches. How can we develop a fuller understanding of the Holy Spirit's power? How can we experience it more completely?

9 How essential is adult water baptism to a person who wants to live as a faithful Christian? How essential is the practice of adult water baptism to the faithfulness of a congregation?

10 How does the Holy Spirit actually work within the life of a human being?

11 Does the Holy Spirit answer the questions for a believer: a.) What would Jesus do? b.) What would Jesus think? c.) What would Jesus say?

4. We Read the Bible Together

As a faith community, we accept the Bible as our authority for faith and life, interpreting it together under Holy Spirit guidance, in the light of Jesus Christ to discern God's will for our obedience.

We know the story of the Triune God through the Bible

The Bible is a very human book. The 39 books of the Old Testament and the 27 books of the New Testament were written by very different authors. The books differ in language, literary form, topics, priorities, and the times they were speaking to. Although the texts have been very well preserved, they had to be copied by hand for many centuries. The manuscripts we have today are copies of the original texts, and they differ in some parts from the original. The Bible is also very human because it is occupied primarily with the fears, the joys, the experiences, the achievements, and the failures of human beings. As Jesus in his incarnation became completely human, we are able to affirm that God speaks to us through Scripture in an entirely human manner.

The Bible is a very divine book. By saying this we make an affirmation of faith that is impossible to prove through human science and logic. The Christian church believes that the incarnated Christ is the Word of God. It believes that Holy Scripture is God's written testimony. These are the great gifts of God to humanity. Without them we do not know anything certain about God. We do not know God's character or saving acts in the past and the future. Jesus has shown us who God is and what God wants to do. And we have reliable information about this, thanks to the Holy Scripture.

The inspiration of the Bible remains a mystery. We do not know for sure how the Holy Spirit guided the writing of the Holy Scripture. Nowhere in the Bible do we get information about mechanisms and techniques. But we do believe that, because of the work of the Holy Spirit, the Bible was written as God wanted it to be.

We also know that the Bible was given to us in languages different from those most of us speak today. Therefore, we depend on translations and the capacity to translate. It is impossible to make perfect translations. Given that human languages live and change, the challenge to provide good translations is a permanent task. To do this, we also need the guidance of the Holy Spirit.

In the Bible we read the reports of witnesses. In order for a book to be considered a part of the New

Testament canon, it had to have been written by a personal witness of the described events, or by someone who interviewed primary source witnesses.

Notice that most of the biblical writers claim to have been part of what they describe. And they have written in such a way that the rest of us can be part of that fellowship: "... and we proclaim to you what we have seen and heard, so that you also may have fellowship with us. And our fellowship is with the Father and with his Son, Jesus Christ. We write this to make our joy complete" (1 John 1:3-4).

We also accept the biblical canon as part of our faith, in the same way as we accept the mystery of its inspiration. From a human perspective, the Bible was established by the people of Israel and the early church. We are not able, nor do we have authority, to defend the Bible. The Bible defends itself as the foundation and authority of the church of Christ, as it has done so well for the last 2,000 years.

Of course, we turn for help to all the disciplines available to have the best translations and interpretation, but we also rely on "canonical interpretation." That means to interpret the Bible with the Bible itself. To those passages which are dark to our understanding, we try to bring light from those passages which are clear and convincing. We also focus on putting into practice those things we understand clearly, rather than being constantly troubled by those passages whose interpretive clarity we have not yet achieved.

This history and this information are the authority for our faith and life

The Bible has authority because we believe that the information it gives is trustworthy. There is no doubt that its goal is to orient our faith and our life. Even though it transmits much historic and scientific information, it uses language, concepts, and world-views accessible to the readers of its time. This does not mean that it has lost authority for our time. Nevertheless, we will use all helpful means of linguistics, history, and science of interpretation to get as full an understanding of the text as possible. And when our logic, or our contemporary sciences, fail to bring us a coherent grasp of the material, we should assume an attitude of humility and self-critique.

We were not present when God created the world, when the Red Sea opened, when the Virgin Mary became pregnant, when Peter and John looked at the empty tomb. Nor do we all agree on how to interpret these written testimonies of God's intervention in history. But instead of making our science and our reason the judges above and over against the biblical text, we should remember to be humble and critical about the capacity of our own science and reason.

The Bible has authority because God himself wanted his will to be known through a written testimony or testament. From the earliest times, God has used scripture writing as a way to be made known through his redeeming interventions in history. God's ethical character became known to the people of Israel through the Ten Commandments written in stone. When Jesus began his ministry in the synagogue of Capernaum, he read the Holy Scripture from the Old Testament. Both testaments state that God wants to write his laws into our minds and our hearts (Hebrews 8:10). Paul wrote to Timothy what the early church applied to the whole biblical canon: "All scripture is God-breathed and is useful for teaching, rebuking, correcting, and training in righteousness" (2 Timothy 3:16).

The Bible has authority because Jesus speaks in it. No, we do not make an idol of a book. Nor do we believe that the Bible fell from heaven. And we do not claim that the word of God became paper. Even though we appreciate every word in the Bible, it tells us itself that Jesus is the Word of God *par excellence* (John 1:14). John, the beloved apostle, states it with clarity: "That which was from the beginning, which we have heard, which we have seen with our eyes, which we have looked at and our hands have

touched—this we proclaim concerning the Word of life. The life appeared; we have seen it and testify to it, and we proclaim to you the eternal life, which was with the Father and has appeared to us" (1 John 1:1-2).

The Bible has authority because the Holy Spirit worked through its authors. In the same way that we accept the incarnation of Jesus, we believe that the Bible is 100% human and 100% divine. As is true about the nature of Jesus, we have to admit that this belief surpasses our rational and logical capacities. The Holy Spirit used normal human beings like us, with their mental and linguistic limitations, within their historical and cultural contexts, and sanctified and guided them in the writing of the Bible (2 Peter 1:21).

The Bible has authority because again and again it was able to reorient the church. The Bible strengthened the church's faith and shaped its everyday ethical life.

The history of the church is also a history of renewal. All authentic renewal emerged thanks to a fresh, intense, and obedient reading of the Bible. That was the case with Francis of Assisi, Martin Luther, with Michael Sattler and Menno Simons. That was the case with John Wesley and Charles Spurgeon, with Florence Nightingale and with Martin Luther King, Jr.

Of course, there also have been many inadequate and literalistic interpretations of the Bible. These have occurred mostly in relation to changing topics of culture, church structure, clothing, and scientific and political concepts.

Literalism, as well as traditionalism, can harm and paralyze the church. That was the case with the Scribes and Pharisees in the time of Jesus. That has been the case from time to time in Lutheran, in Mennonite, in Baptist, and in Methodist churches.

Jesus exhorts us to read the Holy Scripture, searching for the original motivations of the heart of God. That is the reason why the Bible must be read primarily to orient the faith and the life of the church, not to create rituals, traditions, and legalisms.

In order to understand the Bible's meaning for today, we need each other

Congregational interpretation is possible because its members all have the Holy Spirit. That search for biblical meaning which we do together we call congregational interpretation or community hermeneutics.

We believe that when every believer has the Holy Spirit, s/he also receives gifts and produces fruits of the Spirit in order to edify congregational life. "What then shall we say, friends? When you come together, everyone has a hymn, or a word of instruction, a revelation, a tongue or an interpretation. All of this must be done for the strengthening of the church" (1 Corinthians 14:26).

Congregational interpretation is necessary because it is more enriching and less dangerous than an individual attempting it alone. No one has all the gifts or all the necessary knowledge and wisdom. In a congregation we benefit by having women and men, young and old, rich and poor, different temperaments, and representatives of different occupational and professional segments.

A biblical interpretation that emerges "from all" and is directed "to all" will enrich the whole congregation. Such an interpretation can become a protection against abuses by authoritarian individuals. Of course, we need teachers and Bible interpreters who have adequate theological training and the necessary tools for correct interpretation. But biblical interpretation must not become the exclusive right of a few Bible "professionals." Those having the Holy Spirit can cooperate in the interpretation and application of the Holy Scripture.

A good biblical interpretation must conserve and renew. We read the Bible in fellowship with followers of Christ who have read it during the last 2,000 years. It would be arrogant and disingenuous not to be willing to listen to the voice of traditional biblical interpretation. All good traditions grow out of the church's search to be faithful to Christ in its times. But we also have to read the Bible looking to the present and the future. Jesus himself encouraged us to appreciate the old and the new (Matthew 13:52). Our task is to analyze tradition and to reformulate biblical truth and biblical practice in such a way that present and future generations might also understand and be faithful to them.

A good biblical interpretation must be systematic, but also accessible to individuals. The Bible is a collection of epistles, historical narratives, poetry, prophetic words, parables, proverbs, laws, and teachings. In every culture, human minds feel the need to somehow put the biblical teachings into an order that

fits within the logic and understanding of that particular people or cultural group. The church universal also requires some *shared* theological conclusions in order to build unity. Nevertheless, biblical truths must become a faith experience and a faith understanding, lived and experienced in a personal way. To read the Bible in community means arriving at conclusions for all, while also providing expectations for personal behavior.

Our community's biblical interpretation needs the correction and enrichment of the global church. When the Bible is read within a local church, an ethnic group, a culture, or a nation, what emerges is what we call a "local theology." We need this to help us find specific answers to specific situations. This has been true from the earliest Anabaptist congregations, until the most recent Latin American base communities (Matthew 20:1-16). The early Anabaptists read the Bible, wanting to know what it meant to be a follower of Jesus as the Turks invaded Europe and the church called for Holy War. Latin American base communities have wondered how to live Christian solidarity and mutual aid in small agricultural settings the way Jesus would have done it.

But our theologies and our local readings of the Bible cannot be the last word. The body of Christ transcends nationalities, cultures, continents, and denominations. That is why we have to read the Bible as a worldwide community. Many misunderstandings, many prejudices, many confrontations, and even wars between nations with Christian populations, have their origins in the fact that the church has been unable to read and interpret the Bible as the one body of Christ. The "Shared Convictions of Global Anabaptists," developed with the assistance of Mennonite World Conference, are an effort to bring Bible reading and understanding together on a global level.

In order to understand the Bible's meaning for today, we need the Holy Spirit

We need the Holy Spirit to interpret our times in the light of the Bible. The church of Christ has lived through many different times. That continues presently. There have been times of severe persecutions and also times of much public honor. There have been times of economic prosperity and times of poverty. Today some churches live under the rule of totalitarian governments; others live in democracies. Some have lived during anti-Christian ideologies; others when Christianity was the official religion. Some in times of open doors; others in times of closed doors. In all cases, the interpretation of the Bible must relate adequately to the time, the very moment, in which the church is living.

We need the Holy Spirit to interpret our culture in light of the Bible. Every believer is part of a cultural tradition. As all human beings are hybrid because of sin, the same is true of all human cultures. There are good and godly elements in them, and there are also

harmful and sinful elements. We require the Bible and the Holy Spirit to be able to discern what in our cultures must be preserved and rescued, and what requires repentance and change in light of the knowledge of the character and will of God.

We also need the Holy Spirit to interpret our ecclesiological tradition in light of the Bible. The tradition we practice in our churches and in our worship services provides us with peace and security. To honor tradition can mean to honor the forebears of faith. But once tradition loses its significance, and if it does not enrich our understanding of the will of Christ, we are in trouble if we depend on it. Just as every human being needs to have a personal experience of faith and life with Jesus, so also every generation must reexamine its ecclesial tradition in the light of the Bible. The church must feel great liberty to create new traditions, so that the Bible message might become significant for the present and the future.

We need the Holy Spirit to understand the text and setting of the Bible. Of course there are many techniques for doing correct and professional analysis and interpretation of the biblical text. And there are many written resources that help us understand the original historical setting when the Bible stories happened. But the church believes that the Bible is more than an amazing historical and literary text. The Bible text tries to put into human words and concepts realities that belong to God and are spiritual. So we need the Holy Spirit to guide our inductive Bible study and our faithful explorations of the biblical text.

Jesus Christ gives light to intrepreting the Bible

What would happen if we read the whole Bible in the light of the life and teachings of Jesus? Didn't John say that Jesus was the word of God which definitely came to live among us (John 1:14)? What kind of word is this that shines in the darkness without being overcome by the darkness (John 1:5)? What kind of word is this, being so real and visible that it can be seen and touched; so real that one can have fellowship with it; so real that, by looking at it, we already see the Father and his will; so real that it intercedes on our behalf before God (1 John 2:1)?

What would happen if all of our biblical interpretation, and therefore the church's practice and presence in the world, would be centered in the teachings of Jesus? Did not he himself say that he was *the* way, *the* truth, and *the* life? With all respect to those who have another belief, and with all respect to the teachers who preceded and came after him, we who follow Christ do not believe that this is just one more way, just one more truth, just one more form of possible life.

What would happen if we read the whole Bible in the light of the death and resurrection of Jesus? We would not be able to read or understand the Bible without holding uppermost that Jesus has died on the cross. We would not be able to read or understand the Bible without holding uppermost that Christ has risen from the dead. Moses, David, the law, and the prophets would appear from here on in a new light. And the whole life of the apostles and of the apostolic church would center on this fact: "For this very reason, Christ died and returned to life so that he might be the Lord of both the dead and the living" (Romans 14:9). And the logical conclusion for our life and our biblical interpretation would be this: "For Christ's love compels us....And he died for all, that those who live should no longer live for themselves but for him who died for them and was raised again" (2 Corinthians 5:14-15).

What would happen if we would read the whole Bible in the light of the ascension and glorious return of Jesus? The magnificent letter to the Hebrews wants to make clear that the truth of the Jewish Jesus is the truth of God for all times and all people. It begins this way: "God...has spoken to us by his Son, whom he appointed heir of all things....sustaining all things by his powerful word...he sat down at the right hand of the Majesty in heaven" (Hebrews 1:1-3). So the Jesus we adore in the church is the one who holds all power and will come soon to bring the story of humanity to its final goal.

In his message to the Greek philosophers in Athens, Paul maintained that we should interpret all of history from the perspective of the returning Christ, who will come to judge all human deeds (Acts 17:31). And then God's future will begin, when things on earth will take shape the way God imagined. Therefore, should we not already transform "swords" into "ploughs," investing our lives for peace and not for violence? Should we not already interpret all of God's will as expressed in the Bible from the point of view of the messianic age, which is the culmination of human history? After all, we who belong to the tribe of Jesus are already called to live according to the mind of our Lord. That's why the church is attractive—because the heart and mind of Jesus are present there.

We seek to discern and to do the will of God

The Spirit who inspired the biblical authors also wants to lead the community of interpreters to discern the will of God. Thanks to the Holy Spirit, Christians can reach consensus and unanimity. In 1527, when the first Anabaptists got together in the midst of persecutions to search for God's will, they drew up seven articles of faith in the town of Schleitheim on the border of Switzerland and Germany. They were together for several days, praying and studying the Bible. And then they wrote that the Holy Spirit had given them complete unanimity. These seven articles have served as a fundamental biblical and theological basis for consolidating Anabaptist-related churches.

To understand and do the will of God, the community of believers needs processes of discernment. We need the Holy Spirit in order to make ethical decisions which honor Jesus, in the light of the Bible. Changing customs, advancing science and technology, local and global economies, new philosophies and political ideologies, cultural shifts and shared multi-ethnic life, as well as the changing roles of men and women in many cultures, require new answers and ethical decisions.

It is not always easy to define with clarity where the bad is and where the good is. It is not always

obvious whether certain practices belong to the culture of life or the culture of death. We do not always find clear answers in the Bible regarding contemporary ethical questions. That is why the Bible gives the church the authority to "bind" and to "loose" (Matthew 16:19). The community of believers is called to find a way to live ethically in the light of the Bible, through the guidance of the Holy Spirit.

As we obey God's will, we learn to understand better the meaning of the Bible. To discern the church's mission in the contemporary world, we need to discern the will of God. For God, practice is more important than theory. That is why knowing God's will must lead to "orthopraxis"—the correct practice. "Orthopraxis" gives us a better understanding of God's will. The better we obey, the better we understand. Hans Denck, one of the first generation of Swiss Anabaptists, stated it this way: "No one can wholly know Christ, unless he is willing to follow him in his life." A life of obedience is an expression of love toward God. A life of obedience is an expression of trust in the Bible.

The Mennonite church in the Congo has grown rapidly. Today it totals more than 235,000 members in some 1,700 congregations. A woman with theological and pastoral capacities, who is loved and respected in her congregation, declared herself willing to assume the pastoral ministry. This was not part of the tradition of her Mennonite Brethren congregation. Nor is it usual within African tradition and culture that women take positions of public leadership. Additionally, in the Mennonite church of the Congo, as in many Mennonite churches within the global community, there is not a consensus about how to interpret the biblical passages which speak about the ministry of women in the church. But the conference leaders wanted to listen to the voice of the Holy Spirit and give answers to the urgent pastoral needs of their country.

The woman was invited to be ordained for the pastoral ministry in her church. Now there is also a lack of consensus among Mennonite churches concerning the biblical teaching about ordination for ministry. Some believe that ordination is not necessary, because we are all called to serve and we do not differentiate between clergy and laity. Others see ordination as a necessity because it gives a blessing and a public confirmation to church leadership and reinforces God's call through the congregation.

The ministry of women and the rite of pastoral ordination are topics heavily influenced by cultural traditions. But each issue also carries high theological importance. That is why local churches and regional conferences must discern God's will in light of their own situations and cultures, in order to introduce biblical and contextualized solutions.

Study Questions

1. Think of three passages from the Bible which are "very human," as Alfred refers to them.

2. Think of three passages from the Bible which illustrate how it is "a very divine book," as Alfred describes it.

③ Are you reassured by Alfred's suggestion that the Holy Spirit has guided not only the Bible's writers, but also the compilers of the canon itself, as well as the Bible's translators? Do you believe that the Holy Spirit continues to guide today's Bible translators?

④ What do you think of Alfred's idea that we interpret the parts of the Bible that are unclear with related passages that we do understand?

What do you think of his advice to concentrate on practicing what is clear, rather than being bothered by what we can't grasp?

⑤ How do you determine when it is important to pursue the meaning of a passage, and when it is appropriate to humbly accept that it is imponderable?

How do we yield to the authority of the Bible when we can't fully understand it, especially when we live in an atmosphere with a high regard for reason?

6 How do we find, and then maintain, the authority of the Bible in our personal lives today, so that it does shape our faith and our ethics?

7 If the Bible is to reorient the church, how do we make sure that we allow it to do that today? How does your church engage in "congregational interpretation" or "community hermeneutics"?

How might it do that more effectively?

8 Brainstorm about ways your congregation can avoid getting trapped in a too local understanding of the Bible. Brainstorm about concrete ways in which you might be able to benefit from a more global reading of the Bible.

9 What new traditions is your congregation creating that is keeping the Bible significant for you and your children? What ideas do you have about how to have the Bible be a living and shaping force in your congregation?

10 Have you found it to be true that by obeying God's will, you come to understand the Bible better? What is the connection between obeying and understanding?

11 How do we appropriately discern whether an issue is primarily a cultural concern or primarily a "biblical concern"?

5. We Pursue Shalom

The Spirit of Jesus empowers us to trust God in all areas of life so we become peacemakers who renounce violence, love our enemies, seek justice, and share our possessions with those in need.

To be different from the world, we need the empowerment of the Spirit of Jesus

Eleanor and Alan Kreider, as well as Paulus Widjaja, have invested their lives in England and Indonesia to reflect on Christian peacemaking and to practice it in the conflicts within their areas of influence. Together they wrote a superb book called *A Culture of Peace; God's Vision for the Church*. At the Mennonite World Conference General Council meeting in Pasadena, California (USA) in March 2006, they presented the content to the delegates of the global Anabaptist family. There was much agreement about identifying broadly with this theology of peace. This theology applies to situations within the church, within worship and families, and it also explores "peace in the workplace" and "the culture of peace in wartime."

Perhaps the authors' most surprising conclusion is that the culture of peace must begin with, and must always be linked to, evangelism. That is how the empowerment of the Spirit of Jesus is transmitted and received. That is how it all began in the early church. When Peter was sent to Cornelius, God's vision that the church should become a culture of peace began to materialize (Acts 10:44-45).

Because of the work of God in Christ and the active reality of the Holy Spirit, peace is possible between estranged humans.

So in Caesarea, Peter was doing what Jesus had wanted. Led by the Holy Spirit, Peter was making peace with a Roman. The nations of Peter and Cornelius were heading for war. But in the Messiah Jesus the two men were standing together as brothers.

Peter and Cornelius are the nucleus of a new trans-national people of peace. In the future, God's family will be multi-cultural, multi-ethnic. It will be drawn from those in every nation who "fear God and do justice"—and who are open to God's forgiving and reconciling work. This family will be a household of peace in which unreconciled enemies are reconciled, in which unforgiven people are forgiven, and in which they are given a common mission—to share the "good news of peace" with all nations (Kreider, Kreider and Widjaja, 2006, pages 16-17).

To be different from the world, we need to entrust all areas of our lives to God

Only those people with unlimited trust in God are enabled to become real peacemakers. Christians have conflicts in their homes, churches, neighborhoods, and workplaces. The lack of peace often emerges first in the world of our thoughts and emotions. St. Augustine stated it well: "Our heart is without peace until

it finds peace with God." In order for this to happen three things are needed:

- We need to accept that conflicts are normal and inevitable in our lives;

- We need to allow ourselves to hope, knowing that God walks with us and that conflicts well worked through contribute to our growth;

- We need to commit ourselves to prayer, bringing to God our own needs and also those of the other party, asking that God may provide a satisfactory solution for both (James 5:16) (Kreider, Kreider, and Widjaja, 2006, page 179).

Peace has to do with our actions. It is necessary that we go directly to those with whom we disagree (Matthew 18:15-20). We must avoid behind-the-back criticism. We also need a spirit of humility, admitting our own part in a conflict instead of pointing out what others have done (Galatians 6:1-5). It is helpful to be quick to listen and slow to judge. Both sides must be willing to negotiate and to cooperate in favor of a shared solution.

Peace has to do with our attitude toward life. Nothing should distance us from our common foundation, which is Christ and the steadfast love he gives. Sometimes a skilled and gifted mediator can be of help to both sides in a conflict. Many times the community of faith itself can bring relief and restoration. This goes for the local, as well as the regional and global, community. The Bible tells us to trust more in the body of Christ than in the judicial courts to resolve conflicts (1 Corinthians 6:1-6).

The streets of Fresno, California, are among some of the most violent in all of North America. One clear sign of hope emerged when Mennonite deacons and seminary students started organizing mediation services in public schools and working as companions to the local police. The whole city began to learn that Christian churches have skills and practice in conflict transformation and peace-building.

We believe that peacemaking is a blessed duty

Jesus dedicated a special beatitude to "peacemakers" (Matthew 5:9). He declared that the world would call those who do this blessed work "children of God." The letter to the Hebrews relates peacemaking with sanctification, explaining that without peace work and holiness, no one will see God (Hebrews 12:14).

Ricardo Esquivia grew up in a Mennonite orphanage for children of leprosy patients in Colombia. He became a lawyer and has been an important mediator in the violent conflicts between the Colombian FARC and the government. He is profoundly convinced that Christ enables us to become peacemakers. He appealed to the Colombian churches, and to the worldwide Anabaptist family, to transform their churches into "sanctuaries of peace." These sanctuaries would be places where persecuted and anguished people would find refuge, where people would pray and work together in favor of peace.

To work for peace often brings animosity from both sides in a conflict. That is why one cannot do this work without a great trust in God and dependence on God. Peacemaking is a work of faith. Often we do not see the blessing of this work in a lifetime. But trusting that Jesus gave us this mandate and has blessed it, we will strive to be faithful in this duty.

At the Mennonite World Conference Assembly in Strasbourg, France, in 1984, Ron Sider challenged participants to form Christian Peacemaker Teams. Since then, several Teams have gone to areas of conflict in Palestine, Iraq, Central America, Ireland, and elsewhere to fulfill this mandate in the name of Christ and the church.

Dirk Willems, a persecuted Anabaptist of the sixteenth century, saved the life of his torturer who had fallen into a semi-frozen river and was calling for help. Dirk made the decision in a second. He had developed what we might call an instinct or reflex for peace. Faced with danger, he did not attack or flee. His reaction was marked by his fellowship with Jesus and the responses he had learned in the community of believers.

Being a peacemaker must become a habit and a Christian virtue, a part of our culture of peace.

There is no peace without the renunciation of violence

To renounce violence, we need to be empowered by the Spirit of Jesus. The great Swiss theologian Karl Barth gave a considerable boost to the renovation of Anabaptist Mennonite theology in the twentieth century. During the Cold War he spoke and wrote against trusting in arms in order to guarantee peace. Having received 11 honorary doctoral degrees throughout his long life, and stating that he would not take them with him to heaven, he concluded, "The only thing I wanted to achieve in life was to be the donkey that carried Jesus to Jerusalem." When journalists asked him what his major theological discovery was, he answered with the Sunday school song, "Jesus loves me, this I know, for the Bible tells me so."

Because we know that we are loved by Jesus, we can give ourselves the luxury of renouncing violence toward others. Christian ethics can never be anything but the ethic of Jesus. If the church is the body of Christ, the ethic of this body cannot be different than the ethic of its head, which is Christ. That is why Anabaptist Mennonite theology seeks to make the ethics of Jesus relevant for all areas of life and for all the choices we have about how to behave.

Our theology is also convinced that Jesus' ethics and our ethics as a church are good public ethics. Any human being, even one who has not yet resolved to follow Jesus in life, can benefit by applying the ethics of Jesus. Any society can benefit by taking seriously the ethical guidelines of Christ, even without directly confessing Christ. When Jesus identified himself as "the way, the truth and the life," he was stating an ethic that, when practiced, is true for Christians and non-Christians.

Human violence expresses itself in many ways. One of the worst forms is religious violence, when with physical, social, and emotional pressure, people seek to obligate others to believe what they believe. Verbal violence is also reproachable, because hurting words bring denigration and destruction. This is especially true in marriage and family relationships. All the many forms of sexual and inner family violence are incompatible with the Spirit of Jesus. It is essential that we renounce them.

Throughout human history, the rich have exercised a lot of violence toward the poor. And the disadvantaged have frequently reacted with violence. Today we see that the globalized economy has considerable potential to apply violence against weaker societies. Hand-in-hand with globalization comes the imposition of cultural elements. Through their economic and tantalizing power, they can eventually eliminate the values and cultural traditions of less powerful minorities. Media itself can become a driving force for violence when its contents are violent and its commercial strategy is to be violently aggressive.

The most deplorable violence continues to be the use of arms against others. The police often do not know how to do their work without using violence. Authoritarian political structures often use methods of torture and violence to maintain their power. More and more ethnic and religious conflicts seek their solutions with arms. Frustrated minorities choose terrorism. Big economic and political interests continue to cause wars with terrible results.

All these forms of violence cannot claim to have divine approval. They contradict the Spirit of Jesus. We believe that no nation, no ethnic group, no religious or political movement has the right to call upon the name of God, and to pretend to be at peace with Jesus, while taking up arms against human beings. We believe that such attitudes are "pre-Christian." Jesus is clear: "You have heard that it was said: 'Love your neighbor and hate your enemy.' But I tell you: Love your enemies and pray for those who persecute you"(Matthew 5:43-44).

There is no peace without unconditionally loving our enemies

To be able to love enemies, we need the full power of the Spirit of Jesus. The Guidai-Gosode is a territorial group of the war-loving Ayoreos, a tribe who lives in the Chaco regions of Bolivia and Paraguay. They had heard the gospel of Christian salvation in the Bolivian bush region, thanks to some North American missionaries. But they had never heard that Jesus mandates that we love enemies.

After learning to read, and having received a New Testament, one of the Guidai-Gosode discovered the teachings of Jesus in the Sermon on the Mount. In the 1980s he visited his relatives in the Paraguayan central Chaco and shared his discovery. Those listening to him said, "If Jesus calls us to love enemies, then we have to go and find our old adversaries, the Totobie-Gosode (another territorial group of the same Ayoreo nation), who are hostile to any contacts from outside their group and of whom we have killed so many." They chartered a small airplane to find their old enemies. After locating them from the air, they decided to pay them a visit on the ground, even though it required a long walk through the bush.

"Let's not use any arms," said the leaders. "We have killed so many of them, and it might be that some of us will have to give our lives so they might understand that we come in peace and that Jesus has given us love for our enemies." The first minutes of the encounter were very violent. The Totobie-Gosode killed five of the visitors and badly injured four others from the the Guidai-Gosode peace delegation. But when they noticed that their visitors behaved in a completely nonviolent way, the killing stopped, they made peace, and together they returned to the village of the Guidai-Gosode to live and learn with their former enemies.

To love enemies is the most revolutionary part of the Christian message. And it is in this area that the church registers its largest amount of failure and sin. So easily, private interests take over. So easily, pride and the struggle to recover one's offended dignity prevail. So often national identity is stronger than Christian identity. So easily, denominational zeal asserts itself against Christian unity.

We are attached to our material, cultural, and intellectual possessions. We want to defend what is ours, despising, attacking, and hating the one who questions it. We feel humbled if someone else is more successful, famous, or powerful then we are. We lose our security and self-esteem when others criticize, attack, or humiliate us. We cannot love enemies without the Spirit of Jesus giving us the power to do so.

It is good to start loving enemies by practicing with small things. The thoughts and feelings that emerge out of our hearts and minds can take away our peace. We need mental and emotional hygiene. Be alert to the condition of your mind! Pay attention to the state of your heart! If the concept of an enemy gets installed in your mind, it is necessary to rip it out. This enemy might be a member of the faith community. "For where you have envy and selfish ambition, there you find disorder and every evil practice" (James 3:16). It is necessary to delete all images of enemies from our mental archives. If a root of bitterness begins to establish itself in your heart, it is necessary to pull it out. This is true even for bitterness that comes as a result of having suffered injustice. Sometimes one needs to look for professional or community help to become free of bitterness. In any case, what the Bible says is foundational: "See to it that no one misses the grace of God and that no bitter root grows up to cause trouble and defile many" (Hebrews 12:15).

There is no lasting peace without the pursuit of justice

To work without self-interest for the justice that is valid before God, we need the full of power of the Spirit of Jesus. Even if we learn to renounce violence and to love enemies, we must not give up the search for justice.

The church fights for justice, not to get privileges or personal benefits for Christians. It fights for justice because injustice belongs to the "old age of the prince of darkness." Justice belongs to the "new age of the Prince of Peace."

Justice acts as a protective "breastplate of righteousness" in spiritual and social struggles (Ephesians 6:14). Together with the "belt of truth," justice helps us to become "steadfast and to stand our ground." Furthermore, our feet, "fitted with the readiness that comes from the gospel of peace," promote the cause of the kingdom of God (Ephesians 6:15), which at its heart is the cause for truth, justice, and peace.

It is important to note that in the beatitudes, Jesus named the "peacemakers" and the "persecuted for justice" together (Matthew 5:9-10). Biblical justice emerges out of God's righteousness and has economic, social, and even penal dimensions.

Jesus' redeeming work makes us just. That is the central argument which Paul develops in his letter to the Romans. It was biblical truth which triggered the large reform movement of the sixteenth century, when Luther read Romans. Justice was also at the center of reform for the Anabaptists, when they insisted that God's justice must become visible in the life of Christians and the church.

What do we mean when we speak about justice that is "valid before God"? It is a justice "through faith and by faith," through which the righteous live (Romans 1:17). It is at once simple and profound: God declares us just and makes us just. Both things happen through the same saving faith, because faith means trust and also obedience. Both are available to us if we have a relationship of dependence on Jesus.

Christ makes us righteous before God, forgiving all of our sins and delivering us from all condemnation. Christ also makes us righteous through the life of faith, transforming our ethics into lives of obedience, dependence, and trust in him.

Salvation is relationship with Christ. That is the essence of salvation. Its two dimensions, bestowed righteousness and realized righteousness, must never be separated. If one allows them to drift apart, one falls into the error of perfectionism on the one hand, or into moral indifference on the other hand. That is why in Mennonite churches there is rejoicing when persons share that they have found salvation in Jesus. But the church usually waits a prudent amount of time before baptizing these new believers, in order

to observe that the "fruits and evidence of salvation" are present in those making a confession. A change of life, often demonstrated by the restitution of formerly committed injustices, as well as a lifestyle of obedience to Jesus, are signs that lead to water baptism, the external visible act of being incorporated into the family of faith.

The prophetic message of peacemakers includes the prophetic message requesting justice for others. The kingdom of God is a kingdom of righteousness. First, we have to seek for this more urgently than anything else (Matthew 6:33). No, we must not take justice into our own hands. Nor does the church have the political power necessary to implement justice in society from above. It does not even desire powers which are incompatible with the Spirit of Jesus. But with great determination as followers of Jesus, we will pursue and struggle for justice, alone and in community. This struggle requires the same setting aside of one's personal interests as loving enemies demands. It is a struggle to witness and to proclaim.

Neither political ideologies nor secular humanism may nurture this struggle, but, rather, the desire to make the voice of Jesus heard and to make his body visible in the world. That is what Paul did when he confronted Governor Felix: "As Paul discoursed on righteousness, self-control and the judgment to come, Felix was afraid" (Acts 24:25). But the church aims for even more. It wants to live as an example of justice in the middle of its own community. And it wants to do it in such a way that its behavior and attitude become contagious throughout the whole social environment. Jesus called his disciples the "light of the world" and instructed them, "In the same way let your light shine before others, that they may see your good deeds and praise your Father in heaven" (Matthew 5:16).

We had gathered in Santo Domingo at the Latin American Theological Fraternity (FTL). Fiona from Great Britain was with us, sent by the churches of the United Kingdom. She presented us with the "Micah Challenge." Based on what the prophet said (Micah 6:8), she invited us to become part of a worldwide movement seeking to encourage churches to give priority "to acting justly, to loving mercy and to walking humbly with our God."

A little later, Lausanne III, a large worldwide congress on the meaning of Christian missions in the contemporary world, took place in Bangkok, Thailand. Valdir Steurnagel from Curitiba, Brazil, president of World Vision and a member of our Fraternity, gave the central address. His topic was the Micah Challenge. His message, calling us to be a church centered in justice, mercy, and humility, had a profound impact on church delegates from over 100 countries. How glad I was when I recently heard that the Swiss Alliance of Churches adopted the words of Micah as their program of action for the next several years. Humility, mercy, and—justice coming from God—are the basic ingredients for instilling peace that will last.

A Christian culture of peace enables us to share possessions

An important development has occurred within the global Anabaptist family. Pakisa Tshimika from Congo and Tim Lind from the USA together visited many churches worldwide, helping them to discover their gifts and encouraging them to share them within the global church. In their book, *Sharing Gifts in the Global Family of Faith,* which developed out of this experience, they remind us that the Triune God, from creation through Jesus to Pentecost, is a God who shares gifts. The church is a family, a loaf of bread we all share, in which the same Spirit provides many gifts. We receive these gifts in order to share them, so that we all might have abundant life in the global family (Tshimika and Lind, 2003, pages 23-69).

But Tshimika and Lind also identify obstacles to sharing gifts: communication inequities; economic differences; lack of administrative capacity; centralization of decision-making; lack of broad vision; fear of cultural, racial, theological, and other differences; the view that some gifts are more valuable than others; and greed (pages 72-84).

At the end of their book they recommend to all congregations that they become "rich toward God."

"Sometimes it may seem that our churches, in both a real and a figurative sense, are storehouses of wealth—places where human resources are collected and stored, sometimes in ever larger 'barns.' Jesus contrasts keeping our gifts to ourselves with being 'rich toward God.' For a church to be rich toward God, the gifts under the stewardship of the church must be released" (page 108).

In an age of global communication and global networking we might just be in the beginning stage of learning what it means to "share possessions." Nowhere does the Bible tell us to abolish private property. But members of the first church handled their possessions "as if they were not private." And Jesus told the young ruler that he would have to sell all of his possessions. Furthermore, ancient Israel had the institution of Jubilee, which required the whole community to restore equality after every seven years.

Faithful congregations will be very sensitive toward those near them who are in need, as well as those with abundance. As a *global* family of faith we are experiencing the painful recognition that most countries in the Northern hemisphere live with abundance, while many countries in the Southern hemisphere have to survive with extreme material needs. Part of this situation is due to historic and present injustices in the structures of commerce, power, the transfer of technology, and the management of foreign debt. Mennonite World Conference has a Global Church Sharing Fund, one small means of living biblical justice within a world of inequality.

Study Questions

1 Explain, so that you yourself are convinced, the connection between evangelism and peace.

2 Explain, to your own satisfaction, how the story of Cornelius (in Acts 10) demonstrates this connection.

3 How do you believe it is possible for the church ("God's house") to actually include persons who have been at complete odds (for ethnic, cultural, religious, historic, or "bad blood" reasons)?

4 How, practically, do we Christians handle our fears and our memories when we face a conflict, or someone with whom we've had a conflict?

What are the steps to being true peacemakers?

How does true peacemaking become an instinct and a reflex?

5 Explain how when Jesus identified himself as "the way, the truth, and the life," he was making an ethical statement.

6 What stands out most to you in the story of the two groups belonging to the Chaco tribe?

7 How can we prevent our private interests, our pride, our possessions, and our offended dignities from eating away at our peace and unity as Christians? How do we keep even a tiny bit of bitterness from taking root?

8 How does the church decide which injustice(s) to tackle? What specific injustice should your congregation work to make right?

9 What simple but profound explanation does Neufeld give about how we become just and live justly? Do you believe this is true? What evidence have you seen of this happening?

10 What do you think "bestowed righteousness" is? What do you think "realized righteousness" is? What is the danger of having one without the other?

11 In what concrete ways can your church "live as an example of justice in the middle of its own community"?

12 Think of one specific way in which members of your church could handle their personal possessions "as if they were not private."

6. We Worship and Celebrate Together

*We gather regularly to worship,
to celebrate the Lord's Supper,
and to hear the Word of God in a
spirit of mutual accountability.*

Our Christian community loves to get together

We come together so that God may serve us. But why is it necessary to get together, and why do we do it mostly on Sunday? It is because Sunday is the day of resurrection. And the church celebrates this day in the presence of the risen Christ.

But before we who are members of the church are able to bring something to him, God himself wants to serve us in the "service." There are so many things that only he can give us: unconditional acceptance, forgiveness of sin, healing, new dignity, consolation in sorrows, deliverance from anxieties, his own friendship, as well as many old and new friendships, a sense

of belonging, and a call to participate in a big, good, and eternal cause.

We come together to serve God. A true worship service also requires participation from our side. Only then does it become authentic, convincing, and beneficial. We have many ways to serve God. All are answers to and results of God's grace. We serve when we make our time, our gifts, our money, and our capacity to love available to God. Paul calls this "sacrifice of our bodies" a "spiritual worship" (Romans 12:1). We also serve God when we renounce all false idols. We serve when we praise the wonder of God's character and mighty deeds in history.

We come together to prepare for service in the world. God wants to be served through our service to humanity and creation. James explained clearly that "pure and faultless religion" consists in "looking after orphans and widows in their distress and keeping oneself from being polluted by the world" (James

1:27). Jesus himself told us that we can serve him by serving "one of the least of these brothers of mine" (Matthew 25:40). We are to serve the world's physical needs and be a witness to their spiritual needs. Serving others is part of Jesus' mandate to love everyone. Giving witness to salvation through Christ is part of Jesus' commission to disciple all nations. The regular meetings of the community of believers enables us for both services.

Worship is the main reason for Christian meetings

Worship is an attitude of prayer. The Law of Moses strictly prohibited the adoration of any being that was not the true God "in heaven above or in the earth beneath or in the waters. You shall not bow down to them or worship them" (Exodus 20:4-5). And the book of Revelation alerts us not to adore political or national powers: "Who is like the beast? Who can make war against him?" (Revelation 13:4).

But God's deeds are magnified when the church worships and intercedes. The apostles had been imprisoned, and they were forbidden to preach about Jesus. They told their congregation, and the church began to pray: "Sovereign God, you made the heaven and the earth and the sea, and everything in them.... Now, Lord, consider their threats and enable your servants to speak your word with great boldness" (Acts 4:24,29). The prayer of adoration transforms our relationship to God. The prayer of intercession transforms our relationship with our neighbors.

Worship is an attitude of consecration. We have seen that we serve God in the worship service when we make ourselves available to God in an unconditional way. Two aspects come with this authentic adoration. We seek to "sanctify" our life in such a way so that we do not have separate sacred areas and secular areas. And we also renew our covenant with God. What we publicly communicated in our baptism, and celebrate in every Lord's Supper, is also part of all authentic worship: our expressed desire and commitment to be faithful to the Lord.

Worship is an attitude of exaltation. But how can we adore and exalt God? Here we might need to use all of our creativity. Exaltation means saying to God, "You are the supreme! You are the first! You are unique! You are the best!" Women and men of the Bible used all their artistic capacities to exalt God: with music, songs, dance, poetry, narratives, theater, decorations, celebrations, architecture, clothing, culinary arts, tithes, "thank offerings to God and fulfillment of vows to the Most High" (Psalm 50:14).

The celebration of the Lord's Supper and baptism are powerful experiences

From the beginning, Anabaptist churches understood the sacraments to be symbolic, to be "ordinances of Jesus." They did not want to diminish the power of these celebrations; in fact, they wanted to add strength to their meaning. Although they practiced confession of sins, anointing the sick, ministerial ordination,

marriage vows, and blessing children as part of the reforms of the sixteenth century, they did not consider these acts to be formal sacraments. They believed that baptism and the Lord's Supper were visible means of communicating real experiences of divine grace.

As we have seen in Chapter 3, pages 62-64, water baptism conveys at least five messages: receiving the Holy Spirit, dying and being resurrected with Christ, having sins washed away, being incorporated into the church which is the body of Christ, and making a public covenant of faithfulness before God and the church.

The Lord's Supper is a celebration of mutual acceptance and reconciliation. Jesus instituted the Lord's Supper as a sign of the new covenant (Luke 22:20). He celebrated it together with his disciples, sharing bread and wine in a banquet setting. This was Jesus' way of symbolizing God's acceptance and his decision to promote God's kingdom by using unreliable followers just like the disciples and us.

In spite of our sin, God can accept us only because of divine forgiveness. Jesus gave his life and shed his blood to show and make possible this acceptance and this forgiveness. And because God accepts, forgives, and so promotes reconciliation, we also shall forgive, accept, and practice reconciliation. Those who are not willing to forgive, those who are not willing to do the work of reconciliation, have not understood the meaning of the Lord's Supper and should not participate in it. Jesus disapproves of them: "You wicked servant.... I canceled all that debt of yours because you begged me to. Shouldn't you have had mercy on your fellow servant just as I had on you?" (Matthew18:32-33)

The Lord's Supper is a celebration of gratitude and spiritual nurture. Normally we human beings eat to have energy and because we are hungry. In the Lord's Supper, we are reminded that our strength comes from God, from the gift of God's Son in favor of us. Now the bread which we break shows a beautiful symbolism. The many grains of wheat, gone through the mill and the oven of death to the old self, to afflictions, and to persecutions, have been kneaded together in one body, building a unity. The trampled and trodden grapes have become one wine.

But these elements not only symbolize divine nutrition and the unity of the church, they also show what Christ did for us. His body was parted and his blood was shed so that new creation, new peoplehood, new life, could come about.

This fills us with profound gratitude. We remember what Christ did for us. As we participate in the Supper, his historic deed becomes present and is effective within us. During the first Supper, the disciples sang hymns of praise. Today we should express our gratitude likewise.

The Lord's Supper is a celebration of proclamation oriented towards the future. Not the past nor the present, but the future should occupy our minds as we participate in the Lord's Supper, for the church lives more toward the future than from the past. The kingdom of God on earth is anticipation and a bursting forth of the future into the present. That is why we should remember at least two more things every time we celebrate the Lord's Supper: First, to proclaim the death of Christ till he returns (1 Corinthians 11:26). We have evangelistic work to do in light of his expected return. Second, Christ wants us to remember that he is waiting for us so that we can celebrate all together "on that day when I drink it anew with you in my Father's kingdom" (Matthew 26:29).

We get together so that God may speak to us and we might listen

We hear God through the sermon, although the sermon is not the only way to hear God's word. Preaching continues to be a biblical and useful medium through which God speaks to the church. Every good sermon explains a biblical text from the biblical setting and cultures, and then applies the text to the present time and cultures.

A good sermon does not consist only of explanations given by the preacher. It also requires public Bible reading in such a way that the congregation perceives it as the word of God. There should be no sermon without prayer. The preacher or worship leader calls upon our gracious God together with the congregation. And since a sermon seeks to apply God's will to the present situations of the life of the church, the sermon will lead toward intercession for the needs of the church and the world. The church lives in the world and has been sent to the world.

We want to hear God through Bible study. It is the duty of every follower of Christ to know Scripture as Jesus knew it. Many institutions and study guides provide help to do that. In addition to expecting its church leaders to do special studying, the congregation should promote daily reading of the Bible, as well as shared Bible studies, by all believers. A large amount of Bible knowledge can be acquired through personal and devotional studies. And the congregation should not miss offering Bible study in its regular gatherings. Singing and the sermon are not enough to strengthen our faith and to give answers to our daily questions about how to live faithfully as Christians. The Bible is like a big house where we want to live, which we want to know inside out, and from where we want to look at the world.

We want to listen to God through sharing times. "Sing to the Lord a new song!" (Psalm 33:3) The marvelous things God did in the past and does in the present lead to old songs and new songs. We sing them as part of our congregations' singing and in our choirs. In our singing we adore God and proclaim and hear the word of God. The same is also true of sharing times. Congregational meetings, in our homes as well as in our church buildings, need to include time for exchanging testimonies and for honoring God by telling our experiences of his faithfulness in our daily lives. This is also the time when prophetic words can be spoken. These may address the congregational life of the church, as well as the world in which the church lives. As biblical writers gave testimony, so also we want to give testimony to Christ.

We make major decisions together in a spirit of shared responsibility

We share responsibility for our lifestyles. Not all choices in life are personal choices. We have already considered the fact that when we are one body in Christ, we share gifts, both in joy and suffering. This is addressed in a helpful way in the book *Sharing Gifts in the Global Family of Faith* by Tshimika and Lind. (Many of us also experienced this at the Mennonite World Conference Assembly in Zimbabwe in 2003.) To be one body means to be considerate of the other members: "If one part suffers, every part suffers with it; if one part is honored, every part rejoices with it. Now you are the body of Christ, and each one of you is a part of it" (1 Corinthians 12:26-27). Of course we have to avoid social control and respect individual liberty. But both in the local church, as well as in the global family of faith, we need to develop a spirit of mutual responsibility. This includes the needs and lifestyles of *every* member.

We share responsibility for church elections and appointments. Which is the biblical model of church organization? The truth is that such a model does not exist. We might find several models, or at least sketches of different models. But there are at least three constants in the church of the New Testament which have been confirmed in church history: The church needs servant-leaders, the church needs a leadership team, and the whole congregation must share in service and leadership.

The Episcopal tradition (with bishops) has emphasized hierarchical authority and the strong leadership

of individuals. The Presbyterian tradition (with councils of elders) has worked at shared leadership. The congregational tradition has given much authority to the membership assembly of the church.

Anabaptist churches have tried to integrate these three dimensions, believing that the three forms are rooted in scripture. Calling and leadership need to be confirmed by God, as well as by the congregation. Authority must come from "above" and also from "below." In any case, spiritual authority must be based more on spiritual qualities than on having been elected to an office by a majority vote. Nevertheless, these serve to protect and legitimize authority.

Leadership must always be exercised as a team. All leaders in the church must be servant leaders. Spiritual authority is based more on spiritual qualities of service than on having been elected to office. Mutual accountability has to do both with mutual care, as well as with fraternal confrontation. Both contribute to the health of the congregation.

Our theology of discernment, blessing, and ordination of servant leaders seeks to integrate the approval of God and the approval of the congregation.

We also share responsibility for church ministries. All the ministries of the church belong to all the members. Not only the deacons, but also the "apostles, prophets, evangelists, pastors and teachers" are there to "prepare God's people for works of service" (Ephesians 4:11-16). Even though we distribute work according to gifts and possibilities, ministry is still the responsibility of each member. Those who work full-time in church and in missions have the duty to see that the whole church is missional and service-oriented.

Study Questions

1. Alfred suggests three primary reasons for gathering for worship. Does your congregation's worship fulfill all of those?

2. Alfred suggests three attitudes that are a part of worship. Does your congregation's worship include all of those?

3. In what ways does your congregation express worship to God? How many of the artistic expressions listed in the final paragraph of the section, "Worship is the main reason for Christian meetings" (page 110) do you use? Explore how you might incorporate more of the capacities on the list.

4. When in your congregation's gathered times do members exchange testimonies and offer prophetic words? How do you involve everyone in doing this?

5. How does your congregation foster a sense of mutual responsibility in each of its members?

   How does your congregation teach and practice the ideal that "all the ministries of the church belong to all the members"?

6. As demands increase on the time of all of your congregation's members, how does your congregation prevent its mission and service activities from ending up only in the hands of its paid leaders?

7. We Are a Worldwide Family

As a worldwide community of faith and life, we transcend boundaries of nationality, race, class, gender, and language. We seek to live in the world without conforming to the powers of evil, witnessing to God's grace by serving others, caring for creation, and inviting all people to know Jesus Christ as Savior and Lord.

What began small has become global, reflecting the dynamics of the kingdom of God

The Christian cause seeks to penetrate the whole world, and so missions cross many frontiers. It took the early church some time to understand that the cause of Christ is a cause for all humanity. To convince the disciples, the Holy Spirit fell visibly on people outside of their cultural and religious communities, such as the Samaritans (Philip), the gentiles (Cornelius), and also the faithful of the old covenant (in the form of the disciples of John the Baptist, Acts 18:25).

The essence of Christian mission consists of crossing borders. Christ was the first missionary, abandoning heaven and incarnating himself in Galilean culture. Paul argues that Christ came to tear down walls of separation and to kill enmity (Ephesians 2:14). Still today, the church must be a worldwide movement that transcends boundaries of any kind, imitating and continuing the mission of Christ.

The worldwide church of Christ is a body formed by many cells. It is important to remember that none of us is the owner of any church, not even of our local congregation. It is Christ who calls us into *his* church. It is within the Trinitarian fellowship of the Father, Son, and Holy Spirit that we participate if we are part of the church of Christ. Nevertheless, local churches, denominations, national churches,

and regional conferences are important and have a right to exist.

If we are humble we will be able to learn much through fellowshipping and sharing with other denominations. Each church tradition has a beauty and richness, and it is each one's duty to make that accessible to all. It is also impossible to belong to the worldwide church of Christ without being active and participating responsibly in a local church.

Local churches are where the life of the body of Christ is visibly expressed. We could compare these congregations to the individual cells that make up a body. It is true that the many cells of one organism are quite different in form and appearance. But they all have the same genetic code, the DNA, which makes it possible to identify the body of which they are a part. It is here where we have to look for the solution to the many sad conflicts and divisions that have been, and continue to be, present between churches and denominations.

Within a single body, cells do not fight each other unless there is an illness. Thanks to a common genetic code, an organism can function with a great amount of harmony and coordination. In the same way, it does us a lot of good to strengthen our knowledge and awareness of the common Christian code that we carry in our genetics as one worldwide organism, the body of Christ.

Christian community is not limited by nationalities

How important are nationalities within the Christian community? In the Bible we do not find a lot about this topic, but in present church practices, the matter of nationality keeps surfacing. Our personal identity documents certify our nationality; our public rights and duties are ordered by national laws; our civic, cultural, and emotional identities are strongly influenced by our national identity and a sense of patriotism. Normally our local churches associate themselves in a "national conference." Even our theologies tend to have national and continental names: Latin American theologies, German theology, North American theology, the theology of Rome. We find it easy to speak of other nations as "friendly nations," "nations with which we do not have agreements to cooperate," and even "hostile nations."

The Christian message claims that our Christian identity must be stronger than our national identity. But is that possible to achieve? If we look at history, we have to confess that in the past we have committed more errors than victories. When the German nation thought itself to be racially superior, a deep pain lived in the worldwide Mennonite community. Blood affinity and fanatic nationalism had become stronger than a new nationality in Christ. Continental and global associations can be of great help in this matter. Such was the case after World War II when Mennonite World Conference celebrated in Basel in 1952.

We cannot overcome our nationalism if we do not cultivate fellowship with followers of Jesus from other countries and other nationalities. We cannot encourage and correct each other mutually if we do not know the struggles and joys which the family of God lives outside our own country. We cannot be mediators in international conflicts if we do not know the histories, the perspectives, and the needs of the other countries.

During the 1990s, African tribes of Hutu and Tutsi, with evangelical Christians on both sides, faced each other in a war of ethnic extermination. Dalton Reimer, a Mennonite peace researcher, told me once, "It has become more important to belong to the tribe of the Hutu or of the Tutsi, than to belong to the tribe of Jesus."

The church of Christ forms something like a new and different nation right in the middle of all the nations and from all the nations. The apostles talked very openly about the community of disciples as a "holy nation" (1 Peter 2:9). They affirmed that theirs, and our, political identity, "our citizenship, is in heaven. And we eagerly await a Savior from there, the Lord Jesus Christ" (Philippians 3:20).

It is essential that the church, including all local forms of church, never put national interests higher than the interests of the kingdom of God. It is critically important that local churches make a major effort to overcome isolation and to strengthen fraternal ties with local churches in other nations. The mission mandate which the church received from its Lord is that it must be a movement from "all nations to all nations." It is especially necessary during times of international or interethnic conflict that the church forms peace commissions, made up of Christian members representing all the nations or parties involved in the conflict.

Christian community is not limited by ethnicity, race, or language

Different ethnic and cultural traditions reflect something of the diversity and variety which characterize the whole creation of God. And, as does all of creation and humankind, they, too, have their lights and their shadows. They reflect the image of God as well as slavery to sin. Christ wants to restore, purify, and strengthen ethnic identities. They are worthy of being cultivated and protected. But the gospel helps us to assume a self-critical attitude in the light of Jesus. This is especially true when we reflect on the history

of our ethnic group or nation and its interpretation of its past.

Today we are often reluctant to talk about human races and colors of skin. Biological and genetic theories have caused a lot of damage to humanity in the past, and many of those theories lacked scientific authority. The Bible tells us that all human beings have a common bond of origin and dignity. All come from the same family and from the hand of the same Creator, who gave them the breath of life. Therefore, the church is determined to rid itself of any racial prejudice. It will affirm cultural and ethnic identities but reject any "theories of blood," knowing that the "blood of Christ" is the one which makes us equal in the eyes of the heavenly Father and in the community of faith.

The multiplicity and confusion of languages had its origin, according to the biblical reference, in an historical moment when human beings wanted to construct unity so as to put themselves above God (Genesis 11:9). This "Babel-onic confusion" began to be reversed at the moment when God poured out the Holy Spirit. At that time, Jews and non-Jews admitted "...we hear them declaring the wonders of God in our own tongues"(Acts 2:11).

There was a time when some Mennonite churches held tightly and exclusively to the German language. That has changed drastically during the last 50 years. Each human language has a beauty and richness of expression. All are valuable and can be used by the Holy Spirit. It is commendable for Christians to acquire several languages, since knowing only one language makes communication difficult. Being able to communicate in more than one language among members of the faith family strengthens the fraternity, fellowship, and unity of the body of Christ. Milka Rindzinski of Uruguay, Elisabeth Baecher of France, and Rebecca Yoder Neufeld of Canada, as well as many others, put their capacities and linguistic gifts to the service of the worldwide Mennonite family. They serve in the often hidden, but so important, ministry of translation. They make it possible for the global family to function well during worldwide assemblies and through the publication of the multilingual magazine *Courier*.

Christian community is not segregated by class or gender

God has created us different. Even though we share a common human genetic code, every one of us has a particularity. So it is that we are not formally and totally equal, nor would that even be desirable. Christ makes it possible for each individual in the community of faith to develop to her or his maximum potential for growth, self-realization, and service. As in a garden with a variety of flowers, God concedes gifts to everyone, but God does not give the same gifts to all. Nevertheless, all the gifts are important and crucial for the health of the whole body. This is true for natural gifts, as well as spiritual ones.

The biological and emotional differences between men and women have their origins in the Creator. Men and women have been designed to cooperate and to complement each other mutually. This requires a certain mutual subordination (Ephesians 5:21). It also requires critical sensitivity because of the social and cultural expectations that each person receives from his or her culture and tradition. In questions related to gender and role expectations, as elsewhere, the gospel will have a restorative and purifying function. It will strengthen the dignity, participation, value, diversity, and equality of women and men. It will take seriously all the biblical practices and instructions referring to a particular situation, as well as the cultural and historical contexts which are involved. Unity in Christ can be achieved while honoring creational differences: "...for all of you who were baptized into Christ have been clothed with Christ. There is neither Jew nor Greek, slave nor free, male nor female, for you are all one in Christ Jesus"(Galatians 3:27-28).

The same is true for different social classes, groups, and segments. The strong human desire to receive equal treatment, as expressed in the French Revolution, the Bolshevik Revolution, and in many, many

independence movements, finds very limited fulfillment by political means. The faith community gives
strong support to the idea of a lawful State. God, ever
since giving legislation to Israel, has required equality
before the law and impartiality in court.

Social differences in regard to class and status have
several origins. Individual capability, family and cultural traditions, injustices of economic systems, power
abuse, and lack of respect for the law all contribute, so
that most societies are structured according to clearly
visible social classes. Jesus clearly commanded his
disciples that the church shall not imitate this model:
"Not so with you. Instead, whoever wants to become
great among you must be your servant"(Matthew
20:26).

The act of baptism illustrates clearly that there is
just one social class in church: that of forgiven and
restored sinners. The celebration of the Lord's Supper

teaches us that we can each be close to Jesus when we sit around the same table.

In the middle of the world, Christians oppose the powers of evil

When the church wants to stay out of the world, the world will very soon be in the church. The church lives within the world, following a Lord who loves the world but who is completely different from the life and mentality of this world. The church is called to be an alternative force. "Caesar's competition" is the title Bernhard Ott gives to a chapter in his insightful book, *God's Shalom Project*. Ott competently and understandably describes the peace project which God promotes in this world (Ott, pages 111-134). He illustrates how even in ancient times the church was already living the new times of the kingdom of God.

It is crucial that the church maintains a healthy balance. It cannot and must not pull out of the world, because it has been sent to the world. The church cannot and must not conform to the powers of evil, because Christ has defeated them and calls us to overcome evil by doing good.

We confess that as a church, we often have distanced ourselves from the world and its needs. Ricardo Esquivia once told me, "The most difficult thing is to transcend the walls of our church buildings." It is our duty to live completely in the here and now, with an orientation and unconditional loyalty toward that which is beyond.

When the church adapts to the world, it loses its transforming power. What is the world? Where is the world? In theological language, "world" is all human reality that does not accept the lordship of Christ and is not interested in the new times of the kingdom of God and its justice.

The church is often tempted to adapt to the world. Our forms of government and our exercise of power; our priorities in the way we use time, resources, and social connections; our priority of values—all tend to be dominated by the world, which does not yet live salvation in Christ. Jesus emphatically affirmed that we disciples are as different from the world as salt is different from its environment. When salt loses its

power, "it is no longer good for anything, except to be thrown out and trampled under foot" (Matthew 5:13).

This world needs change and conversion. Not only the church, but many thinkers and leaders as well, are convinced that profound transformations in humankind are necessary. The prophet Micah's great image of swords being transformed into ploughs has inspired the United Nations, which adopted it as its official emblem. Sometimes Anabaptist Mennonite churches have made common cause with peace organizations that pursue the same goals which the prophet Micah announced. Menno Simons declared that the church is already this place where arms of war are being transformed into instruments of peace. This desire for peace is shared by many who do not yet belong to the community of faith.

In 1889, the countess of Prague, Bertha von Suttner, inspired by the prophet Micah, published her novel *Put down the Arms*. As in the United States, where the novel *Uncle Tom's Cabin*, written by another female pacifist, produced a favorable atmosphere to abolish slavery, so the book by Countess Bertha inspired peace movements in Europe. Together with her wealthy friend Alfred Nobel, Bertha invested the rest of her life in promoting peace through several organizations, in the middle of a world ready for war. Thanks to her inspiration, Alfred Nobel established the famous Nobel Peace Prize in his will. In 1905, Bertha received the Nobel Peace Prize.

As followers of Jesus, we believe that even more radical changes are possible than those promoted by peace prizes. When Menno Simons talked about the "children of God" who already transform swords into ploughs, he was referring to those who identify completely with Jesus. John Driver, a much loved Bible teacher in Latin American Mennonite churches, calls the church in its relation to the world a "Christian counter-movement."

The majority of Christian theologians are convinced that Christ wants to transform cultures for the better. But Christ does that only through the visible community of his followers. Spiritual, ethical, and social transformations manifest themselves and are lived in real human communities. It is in the church where Christ is being found. And it is Christ through his church who brings transformation.

God's world fallen into sin needs dialysis. What, then, is the relationship between the gospel of Christ and human cultures? This is an urgent question for the life of the church in its testimony to the world, as well as for transcultural missions. The gospel that does not take culture into account becomes something foreign, superficial, and insignificant. If the gospel identifies completely with a culture without questioning and redeeming it, the same thing happens.

I would like to propose the dialysis model for questions of gospel and culture, Bible and contexts. Dialysis is the work that a kidney does with blood. Our cultures are like blood which gives life to the whole body. The gospel revealed in the Bible is like a kidney. It extracts the toxic and destructive elements out of the blood. The kidney, together with the lungs, provides the blood with oxygen and nutrition for life. This is what Christ and the gospel—lived by the church—want to do with the cultures of both those within and outside of the faith community.

In the middle of the world, Christians witness to the transforming grace of God

Many advocates of change end up in great frustration. And those who believe in them become disappointed. But since divine grace broke into our lives, we know that change is possible. Christian faith looks for the source of change outside of human reality. Jesus invites in a special way those who are frustrated and tired, because it is his grace that brings them the desired relief. Christian witness is authentic only when it points toward God and God's work of grace.

The new covenant of grace is better than the covenant of law. Even though the church of Christ is closely linked and indebted to the faith of Abraham and the covenant God made with Israel, the New Testament tells us that the old covenant can be misinterpreted in a dangerous way. This happens when people try to follow the law and do good works in order to establish their own merit, instead of recognizing and honoring divine grace.

Jesus and the apostles interpreted the prophets of the Old Testament by concluding that in their time, they were witnessing the fulfillment of the promise of the new covenant of grace. God said, "I will put my law in belivers' minds and write them in their hearts...and I will remember their sins no more" (Hebrews 8:10-12). Paul credits this special power to the Holy Spirit: "...in order that the righteous requirements of the law might be fully met in us, who do not live according to the sinful nature but according to the Spirit" (Romans 8:4).

Grace is a work of God. We can only witness about it and be used by it. Thanks to God's grace, we are able to have hope.

Grace is not something we can do, but that which we are unable to do. The Bible is even more radical: The weaker and more useless we feel, the better God's grace can act in our lives. This is a great comfort as we engage in relief, as well as evangelistic, service. There are no social situations so wretched that the grace of God cannot transform. There is no human misery so desperate that the grace of God cannot transform. There are no human sins so big that the grace of God cannot forgive. There are no human failures so terrible that God's grace cannot restore.

Because God is love, we want to live a life of service

God dignifies human labor. It is not a curse to work. Work is not a result of Adam's sin, because work was present before sin appeared.

God the creator claims to be the most joyous and dedicated laborer. Day and night God cares for creation and restores fallen humanity. Human labor needs to be dignified in the light of divine labor. Much human labor is, in a certain way, a service of love to one's neighbor because it produces necessary goods for the life and happiness of others. Work that offers no service perspective to humanity serves a culture of death and does not deserve to be done.

A life of service gives satisfaction. We have been created to want to see meaning in our lives. Without a sense of meaning, life becomes superficial and desperate. Those who invest their lives in service for others speak of a high level of satisfaction. We serve Christ serving others. A culture of service is necessary to respond to so many urgent human needs: lack of health, education, food, and family; spiritual and economic poverty; the need for companionship, comfort, and joy.

A life of service has transforming power. "He who does not serve is of no service," Rudolf Duerksen, head of Mennonite Voluntary Service in Paraguay, used to say. This is confirmed by the experience of many young people, including my own children. Their time of service transforms them. To live with the poor and marginalized, to be exposed to their everyday reality, profoundly impacts the lives of those who seek to serve. International Mennonite programs of service, such as MCC, Pax, Trainee, and Christian services, testify to two things: Service brings blessings to the needy, and service transforms those who serve for the better.

Because we have hope, we want to care for creation

Creation is not doomed to becoming a holocaust. But many human groups, including Christians, treat creation that way, subjecting it to irresponsible deforestation, exploiting the soil, polluting the air, severely damaging the ecological balance, being negligent about managing waste. All of this is aggression toward creation which God the Creator has entrusted to our care.

For a long time we did not even have a theology of ecological care. Even worse, some preached that this earth is doomed for destruction anyway. But as I understand it, the Bible tells us something else. Even though there are prophetic words about terrible natural disasters to come, God's promise to Noah not to fully destroy life on earth will be fulfilled. Remember the rainbow, the sign of this covenant. The book of Revelation indicates that God wants to renew the earth and to one day unite it with heaven in the new creation (Revelation 21:1-3). How that will come about remains a mystery.

In our Christian spirituality we have to avoid worshiping creation instead of the Creator (Romans 1:25). This is the error of Pantheism and of Mother Earth worship. But we can honor God by honoring

creation, because it reveals something of the wisdom, the power, and the majesty of God. Many Psalms sing about this and the apostle Paul affirms it in Romans 1:20.

The way in which we use creation we borrow from our children's future. Responsible Christian ethics will always consider the coming generations. We do not know when Christ will come or when the day of the last judgment will arrive. We have to be prepared to face eternity at any moment. But this reality must never be used as an excuse to justify abusing creation. The future of social ethics and global politics, as well as the future of ecology, are responsibilities we have to assume today, thinking of our children and grandchildren. That is what the Psalmist already proposed: "Great is the Lord and most worthy of praise; his greatness no one can fathom. One generation will commend your works to another, they will tell of your mighty acts" (Psalm 145:3-4).

Because we have faith, we invite all people to know Jesus Christ as Savior and Lord

The invitation to receive the Good News comes from Christ himself. There is no doubt: Authentic Christian faith is contagious. And it must be that way. It happened during the times of great revival when so many churches were born and renewed, including the Anabaptist movement. But even more so in the early church and the times of the Apostles, the cause of Jesus extended like a fire, as the book of Acts tells us. Jesus himself wanted it to be that way.

But we are wrong if we consider ourselves to be able to save people. We cannot even convert ourselves. The call to conversion, the invitation to know him, comes from Christ himself. He calls us to his fellowship; he calls us toward his church. Human beings are able to respond and to assume responsibility for their choices. Like John the Baptist, we are able to lead people to Christ and to point toward him. With John we will rejoice when they do not follow us, but the good master himself. And with Paul we will be eager to become models of discipleship, so we can say: "Follow my example, as I follow the example of Christ" (1 Corinthians 11:1).

Christ invites us to know him through his church. It is always fascinating to hear how people came to know Christ. In most cases, a Christian helped them. Actually, there usually are many and different persons who cooperate in helping someone learn to know Christ. The experience tends to differ from case to case. For

many, at a certain decisive moment in their past, they made a decision, confessed their sins, spoke a prayer of consecration, confessed Christ as Lord and Savior—and from that moment felt assured of salvation. For others, the experience is more of a process. It might have begun with Bible instruction in a Christian home and with church experiences during childhood. There may have been some crisis which ended with the person making a firm and determined commitment.

The form and moment of conversion are not as important as the result. It is not that critical to know when and where one was born; the crucial thing is to be alive. The result of an authentic knowledge of Christ is new life through grace and forgiveness, confessing Jesus as Savior, and following him in life as Lord. It would have been impossible for us to come to know Christ without his church. All we know about him comes from his church, who lives the Scriptures. Those who helped us to know him were part of his church.

The faith experience has both an individual and a community dimension. To know Christ always includes both dimensions. It is impossible to be an active member of the faith community without having had personal experiences of faith. And it is of no use to cultivate an individualized spiritual life, if we do not express it in interpersonal relationships within and outside of the church.

The image of the body and its cells is also a parallel to conversion and spirituality. The life and genetics of every cell relates to the life and genetics of the body as a whole. Healthy cells give life to a body. A healthy body strengthens every cell. So it is that evangelism and Christian missions reach out to individuals, but are equally concerned with establishing healthy churches. It is those churches which will fulfill holistic missions in their communities.

Study Questions

1. Try to name all the borders that your congregation crosses in its various missions. What borders does the national church to which your congregation belongs work across?

2. How have those activities enriched your national church's and your congregation's faith life?

3 How do baptism and communion level social differences?

4 Do you agree with Alfred's statement, "When the church wants to stay out of the world, the world will very soon be in the church"?

5 How does the church not lose its balance? How does it not remove itself too far from the world, on the one hand, or be drawn into subtly adapting or conforming to the world, on the other hand? What monitors and safeguards can it use to check itself?

6 What evidence can you point to of the church ("Christ's visible community of his followers") transforming culture for the better?

7 Give a concrete example of the church functioning like a kidney.

8 Name particular and recent signs of God's grace that you have witnessed, both in your own life and in the world around you.

9 Think about your own work or vocation. In what specific ways is it a service of love?

10 Explain the connection, as you understand it, between hope and caring for creation.

11 Do you agree that "the faith experience has both an individual and a community dimension"? In what ways has that been true for you?

History Matters

In these convictions we draw inspiration from Anabaptist forebears of the sixteenth century, who modeled radical discipleship to Jesus Christ. We seek to walk in his name by the power of the Holy Spirit, as we confidently await Christ's return and the final fulfillment of God's kingdom.

We are thankful for a "cloud of witnesses"

Anneken Jans was a young widow in the Netherlands. Although she had not done theological studies nor held leadership positions in the church, she was arrested for singing an Anabaptist hymn while using public transportation. In jail she wrote a letter-testimony to her 15-month-old son. She encouraged him to "walk in the way of Jesus and to drink the bitter cup which so many members of the faith community had to drink; to go through the narrow door and walk the way of life, which is Jesus; to search in Scripture and flee from the darkness of the world; to fear God more than human beings and to confess Jesus in front of man; to honor God with good works, so the light of the gospel might shine; to share with the brothers and sisters in need and always have a conduct according to the gospel, knowing, that we are trees planted by God in the New Jerusalem." On the day of Anneken's execution, January 24, 1539, a pious bread baker saved her son, together with her written testimony. So it was preserved for us till this day. Anneken's son later became mayor of the city of Rotterdam, although we do not have evidence that he accepted the faith of his mother (Oyer and Kreider, pages 38-39).

Our Anabaptist forebears, thanks to their Bible reading, had the courage to explore new ways. Arnold Snyder summarizes their heritage in three categories:

- Concerning Anabaptist doctrines, they insisted that the church must be visible, being formed by believers born from the Spirit and centered on Christ. All believers must know the Bible, own their own faith, and be able to explain and defend it biblically. The church becomes visible because its members are obedient disciples of their Lord and Master Jesus Christ, known for their repentance, rebirth, and new life (Snyder, pages 20-21).

- Concerning Anabaptist ordinances and ritual practices, they were convinced that baptism, church discipline, the Lord's Supper, and foot-washing served to make these doctrines visible (pages 35-36).

- Concerning Anabaptist discipleship, Snyder discerns three important ethical aspects of a "holistic spirituality": to speak truth, share possessions, and practice pacifism (pages 37-47).

Snyder surprises us with the affirmation that following Christ means to maintain balance.

There has been only one human being who achieved perfect balance, and he was the Son of God. As followers of Jesus we can and should look to the worldwide community of faith....We can learn from Pentecostal and charismatic Christians that obedience to church rules and orders is no substitute for nurturing and cultivating a vital life of the spirit.

The Anabaptists wished to establish a careful balance between salvation as a gift of God and a life of obedience as a response to God's grace. In some cases, the Anabaptist pendulum swung far to the side

of works and over-valued the works of discipleship. At those times, Martin Luther's insight provided a helpful corrective. Discipleship and obedience are, in the final analysis, also gifts of grace (pages 51-52).

The important Anabaptist heritage, which till this day should be held in high esteem, is the search for a holistic gospel, which "refuses to allow salvation and the spiritual life to be separated from a life of obedience and discipleship. The two belong together. Here is the particular seed, fruit, and vintage we have inherited from the Lord and our parents in the faith" (page 52).

We want to walk with Jesus as they did

Jesus points out the danger of "decorating the tombs of the prophets and the monuments of the righteous" without being willing to identify with the way they

walked (Matthew 23:29). That warning is still valid for us in our relation to the first Anabaptists. Our forebears in faith, the same as other Christians of their time, also committed many errors. It is our responsibility to admit them, seek restitution, and not repeat them. In part, a process to heal the memories of the sixteenth century has begun with the recent Catholic-Mennonite dialogues. But the Anabaptist movement has also left us a legacy of courage and faithfulness. This is a heritage which must be honored with deeds.

A blind and fanatical confessionalism and denominationalism is absurd. We do not follow the Anabaptists; we do not follow Menno Simons. We follow Jesus Christ. That is true also for other Christian denominations. Neither Luther nor Calvin nor Zwingli nor other important theologians of the church of Christ expect that we should follow them. But as they have followed Christ, they have provided models, exhortations, and inspiration for us that are very helpful today.

Some churches in our worldwide fellowship today live in situations very similar to those of the Anabaptists in the sixteenth century. They are small minorities, sometimes persecuted, sometimes marginalized, sometimes despised. For other churches within our faith family, the social situation is completely different. They live in nations with law and order, including religious freedom. They enjoy high esteem for their pacifist attitudes, their economic efficiency, and academic excellence. In some countries, members of these churches are encouraged to cooperate in civil and political responsibilities.

Rarely can we apply the Anabaptist legacy directly to contemporary situations. But that legacy includes those believers' theological understandings and priorities, and their models for ortho-praxis and holistic spirituality.

The kingdom of God will prevail

We do not yet see God's kingdom clearly prevailing. In *God's Shalom Project,* Bernhard Ott reminds us of what Paul says in Romans 8: The new creation of God is still in the delivery stage. For Ott that means at least three things:

- The new has begun. New life has been conceived and is already underway. Three events guarantee this: Jesus is the promised Messiah, Jesus completed his redemptive work and lives, and Jesus has poured out his Spirit.

- The new is not fully present. Individual renewal and community renewal are not achieved instantaneously. They are processes that again and again require painful experiences, as in any birth process.

- But the goal is in sight. The Holy Spirit is a down payment toward the coming world. Consequently, we live in the tension of a guaranteed hope that has not yet been fulfilled.

Ott reminds us that Christians are not always able to achieve a balance in the tension between these two polarities. Sometimes the "old world" becomes so dominant for them that they seem to forget the reality of the resurrection of Christ, as well as the coming of the Holy Spirit in Pentecost. They live as if the kingdom of God has not yet come.

But there is also the other extreme. There are Christians who believe that they have completely achieved the goal already. They want to have it all, and right now, too: health, prosperity, total liberation from sin, paradise on earth. Sooner or later they experience bitter truth. Sin, illness, and personal limitations are still real (Ott, pages 120-123). Those are the "next to last words." But we know that Jesus and his kingdom will have "the last word."

The church in the power of the Holy Spirit will continue to be the showcase and vanguard of this kingdom—not more, not less. Menno Simons never ceased teaching that we followers of Christ have abandoned "Babel" and have entered the "New Jerusalem." God wants to show the whole world the arrival of his kingdom. Therefore, the church has to live the justice of this kingdom in a public and understandable way. As a good showcase invites everyone to buy, so the

church must invite everyone to acquire the jewels and richness of all that Christ offers.

But the followers of Christ must also endure a "battle of the pacifists" (Ephesians 6:10-20). While avoiding false concepts of "spiritual warfare," they know that they are the vanguard sent by the King as "sheep among wolves" (Matthew 10:16). But because the Lamb of God has overcome the world, they are sure that the victory of the Lamb is also the victory of the church.

Our joy will be complete on that day when Christ returns. We have said that the church lives more toward the future than toward the past. The return of Christ, who as a groom comes to take home his bride, is a powerful moving force of hope. It is an article of faith which seems pretty ridiculous to rational minds. And, of course, many generations preceding us have waited for this event. But all these unknowns dare not weaken our faith. Because we have confidence in the promises Christ himself made, they make a lot of sense. God will not leave his redeeming work unconcluded.

The final vision of Revelation 21-22 tells us about a new heaven and a new earth, as well as the coming down of the New Jerusalem. God will make new what we know (earth). And God invites us to participate in what we don't know (heaven).

God will not allow human injustice to be tolerated in eternity. Jesus will not disappoint his disciples who faithfully work to multiply their received talents, so that they might present a positive balance when he returns.

The return of Christ will bring immeasurable joy to his church. The return of Christ will complete our salvation. The coming of Christ will make real what we still are praying for: "May thy kingdom come, may thy will be done, as in heaven so on earth."

Study Questions

1 Who is in your "cloud of witnesses"?

2 In what ways is the church visible, and effectively so, in the particular world in which you live?

3 How does the church help you to maintain "a careful balance between salvation as a gift of God and a life of obedience as a response to God's grace"?

4 In what ways, if at all, do you benefit from the choices and practices of the early Anabaptists?

5 How do you not give up hope that "the kingdom of God will prevail"?

Readings and Sources

Hussein, Bedru and Lynn Miller. *Stewardship for All? Two believers— one from a poor country and one from a rich—speak from their settings.* New York, NY: Good Books, 2007.

Kreider, Alan, Eleanor Kreider, and Paulus Widjaja, *A Culture of Peace; God's Vision for the Church.* New York, NY: Good Books, 2005.

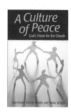

Lapp, John and C. Arnold Snyder, eds. *Anabaptist Songs in African Hearts: A Global Mennonite History, Africa.* New York, NY: Good Books, 2006.

Lapp, John and C. Arnold Snyder, eds. *Churches Engage Asian Traditions: A Global Mennonite History, Asia.* New York, NY: Good Books, 2011.

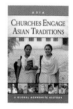

Lapp, John and C. Arnold Snyder, eds. *Mission and Migration: A Global Mennonite History, Latin America.* New York, NY: Good Books, 2010.

Lapp, John and C. Arnold Snyder, eds. *Seeking Places of Peace: A Global Mennonite History, North America.* New York, NY: Good Books, 2012.

Lapp, John and C. Arnold Snyder, eds. *Testing Faith and Tradition: A Global Mennonite History, Europe.* New York, NY: Good Books, 2006.

Ott, Bernhard. *God's Shalom Project; An Engaging Look at the Bible's Sweeping Story.* New York, NY: Good Books, 2004.

Oyer, John S. and Robert S. Kreider. *Mirror of the Martyrs.* New York, NY: Good Books, 1990.

Snyder, C. Arnold. *From Anabaptist Seed; Exploring The Historical Center Of Anabaptist Teachings And Practices.* Kitchener, ON: Pandora Press, 1999.

Tshimika, Pakisa and Tim Lind. *Sharing Gifts in the Global Family of Faith; One Church's Experiment.* New York, NY: Good Books, 2003.

About the Author

Alfred Neufeld is a Mennonite theologian from Paraguay. An ordained minister, he has spent most of his professional life teaching and building up educational institutions.

Neufeld is currently Rector (President) of the Universidad Evangelical del Paraguay, a Protestant university owned by the Anglican, Baptist, Presbyterian, Disciples of Christ, Mennonite, and Mennonite Brethren churches of Paraguay.

He is also a visiting professor at the Basel-Bienenberg Mennonite Seminary in Switzerland.

About the Photographer

Merle Good is a writer, publisher, and photographer from Lancaster, Pennsylvania.

His books have sold more than 800,000 copies. His Off-Broadway play, "The Preacher and the Shrink," premiered at the Beckett Theatre in New York in 2013. His Op-Ed essays have been published in *The New York Times,* *The Washington Post,* and *The Los Angeles Times.*

Good has volunteered as a photographer, writer, and fundraiser for Mennonite World Conference for more than 30 years.

METHOD OF PAYMENT

❒ Check or Money Order
  (*payable to **Skyhorse Publishing** in U.S. funds*)

❒ Please charge my:
  ❒ MasterCard   ❒ Visa
  ❒ Discover   ❒ American Express

\# _____

Exp. date and sec. code _____

Signature _____

Name _____

Address _____

City _____

State _____

Zip _____

Phone _____

Email _____

SHIP TO: (if different)
Name _____

Address _____

City _____

State _____

Zip _____

Call: (212) 643-6816
Fax: (212) 643-6819
Email: bookorders@skyhorsepublishing.com
(do not email credit card info)

Group Discounts for

What We Believe Together
ORDER FORM

If you would like to order multiple copies of
What We Believe Together by Alfred Neufeld for
groups you know or are a part of, please email
bookorders@skyhorsepublishing.com or fax order
to **(212) 643-6819**. (Discounts apply only for more than
one copy.)

Photocopy this page and the prior one as often as
you like.

The following discounts apply:

1 copy	$12.99
2-5 copies	$11.69 each (a 10% discount)
6-10 copies	$11.04 each (a 15% discount)
11-20 copies	$10.39 each (a 20% discount)
21-99 copies	$9.09 each (a 30% discount)
100 or more	$7.79 each (a 40% discount)

Prices subject to change.

Quantity   *Price*   *Total*

____ copies of *What We Believe Together* @ _____ _____

Shipping & Handling (add 10%; $3.00 minimum) _____

TOTAL _____